SEMINAR STUDIES IN HISTORY

# War in Europe 1939–1945

**SEMINAR STUDIES IN HISTORY**

General Editor: Roger Lockyer

# War in Europe 1939–1945

## Anthony Wood

**LONGMAN**

London and New York

LONGMAN GROUP UK LIMITED
Longman House, Burnt Mill, Harlow, Essex CM20 2JE, UK
and Associated Companies throughout the World.

Published in the United States of America
by Longman Inc., New York

First published 1987
ISBN 0 582 35455 2

*Set in 10/11 pt Baskerville Roman. Linotron 202
Produced by Longman Group (FE) Limited*
Printed in Hong Kong

---

**British Library Cataloguing in Publication Data**

Wood, Anthony, 1923–
  War in Europe 1939–1945. – (Seminar
  studies in history)
  1. World War, 1939–1945 – Campaigns –
  Western   2. World War, 1939–1945 –
  Campaigns – Eastern
  I. Title     II. Series
  940-54'21     D756
  ISBN 0-582-35455-2

---

**Library of Congress Cataloging in Publication Data**

Wood, Anthony.
  War in Europe, 1939–1945.
  (Seminar studies in history)
  Bibliography: P.
  Includes index.
  1. World War, 1939–1945 – Campaigns – Western.
2. World War, 1939–1945 – Campaigns – Eastern.
3. World War, 1939–1945 – Campaigns.   I. Title.
II. Series.
D756.W66  1986     940.54'1     86-7326
ISBN 0-582-35455-2

# Contents

*Contents*

# List of maps

# Acknowledgements

We are grateful to the following for permission to reproduce copyright material:

Author's agents on behalf of C. & I. Publications Ltd for an extract from pp. 78–9 *The Second World War* Vol. 2, by Winston S. Churchill, Copyright 1949 by C. & I. Publications Ltd; Collins Publishers for extracts from *Turn of the Tide* by Arthur Bryant; the Attorney on behalf of Margaret Truman Daniel for an extract from *Years of Decision* by Harry S. Truman, Doubleday & Co. Inc., 1955; the Controller of Her Majesty's Stationery Office for extracts from *Grand Strategy* Vols 3 (part 1) and 4, 1964 and 1970 by Gwyer; Michael Joseph Ltd for extracts from *Panzer Leader* by Heinz Guderian, trans. Constantine Fitzgibbon; author's agents for extracts from *The Other Side of the Hill: Memoirs* by B. Liddell-Hart, Cassell & Co Ltd; author's agents and Harper & Row Inc. for an extract from pp. 519–20 *Roosevelt and Hopkins: An Intimate History* by Robert Sherwood.

Cover: Jon (full name William John Philpin Jones) cartoon, c. 1944. Source: Imperial War Museum, London.

# Seminar Studies in History

Founding Editor: Patrick Richardson

## Introduction

The Seminar Studies series was conceived by Patrick Richardson, whose experience of teaching history persuaded him of the need for something more substantial than a textbook chapter but less formidable than the specialised full-length academic work. He was also convinced that such studies, although limited in length, should provide an up-to-date and authoritative introduction to the topic under discussion as well as a selection of relevant documents and a comprehensive bibliography.

Patrick Richardson died in 1979, but by that time the Seminar Studies series was firmly established, and it continues to fulfil the role he intended for it. This book, like others in the series, is therefore a living tribute to a gifted and original teacher.

*Note on the System of References:* A bold number in round brackets (**5**) in the text refers the reader to the corresponding entry in the Bibliography section at the end of the book. A bold number in square brackets, preceded by 'doc.' [**doc. 6**] refers the reader to the corresponding item in the section of Documents, which follows the main text.

ROGER LOCKYER
General Editor

# Foreword

The first purpose of this book is to sketch a very brief outline of the Second World War, as it affected the European continent. Naturally, from the end of 1941 the Japanese advance created a vast second theatre of operations in the Pacific and South-East Asia, and, as will be seen, strategic decision-making in Europe was bound to be influenced by this other war in the Far East. Nevertheless, the nature of the campaigning there and the geographical areas involved were so different that they really require separate treatment, and it seemed justifiable in the interest of simplicity and clarity to deal here purely with the European war.

The second purpose is to move away from the Whig interpretation which assumes an inevitable victory for the Allies over the Axis Powers of Germany and Italy. Accordingly, in the Assessment section I have tried to examine the moments of decision, when events could have turned out very differently. This is not merely from the point of view of victory or defeat. After 1939 the map of Europe was put into the melting-pot; the shape and nature of the new one to emerge in 1945 depended upon the relative positions of the armies at the end of the war, and these in turn were governed by strategic decisions taken earlier in the course of that war.

In a book of this size, these two aims are bound to mean a highly compressed and analytical approach, and this may obscure the fact that the raw material of these extraordinary years consisted of the millions of servicemen and civilians, men, women and children, who throughout this time died from shooting, shelling, bombing, burning or drowning. Their names do not live for evermore and they did not always die most gloriously. They were just unlucky to be born when and where they were, and it is the hope of the author that younger readers of this book will never be at the mercy of the circumstances that they knew.

Anthony Wood<br>
Winchester 1986

# Part One:   The Background

## 1   The Opposing Forces

The Second World War began in September 1939 when Hitler, the ruler of Germany, invaded Poland, and Great Britain and France declared war on Germany in support of their Polish ally. Within a month Poland had succumbed to the German army; by June 1940 France had been overrun and surrendered, and Hitler, now joined by Mussolini's Italy – the two of them representing what were known as the Axis Powers – controlled Europe from the Pyrenees to the border that he shared with Russia in eastern Poland. Under Winston Churchill the British government resolved to continue the fight, and gradually the implications of the struggle spread across the world. From the beginning the antagonists had wrestled over the command of the oceans and the air, and the entry of Italy into the war soon made Mussolini's Italian empire a theatre of operations in north and east Africa. In June 1941 Hitler invaded Russia, and in December 1941 Japan, after launching her own attack on the United States in the Pacific, began her advance into south-east Asia. Thus, when Germany and Italy threw in their lot with Japan, the war had indeed become a world war.

In Europe it all ended in May 1945, when the Anglo-American forces and the Russian Red Army met in the middle of Germany. By that time a trail of destruction had spread up the length of Italy, throughout most of Normandy and the southern part of the Netherlands, and across the plains of Russia and Poland, while the major areas of Germany had been shattered by a prolonged bombardment from the air. The number of casualties had been appalling – a total of more than thirty million, of which Russia suffered about two thirds. The Germans themselves had lost three and a half million servicemen and one and a half million civilians, dead or missing. And for the survivors normal life on the Continent had completely disintegrated. The Allies were coping with seven million prisoners of war; another seven million displaced persons, mostly Slavs brought to Germany for forced labour, were housed in camps of wooden huts; and eventually some twelve million Germans, willingly or otherwise, were to move westwards from

1

eastern Europe, where Russia was in a position to control the new forms of government and society to be established there.

The forces that faced each other at the beginning of this conflict in September 1939 varied greatly in size and quality. Traditionally Great Britain had had a very small army and the extent to which it had been run down in the inter-war years meant that initially she had only six regular divisions available. By the time of the German attack on the western Allies in May 1940 she had in all some ten divisions in France and there were plans for an eventual fifty-five by September 1941. The French had some sixty-five active divisions, including one armoured and two mechanised, and by May 1940 their total stood at about ninety-four. At the beginning of the war the Germans could only rely on fifty-two immediately active divisions, although within a few weeks this had been increased to 103 divisions of 3,700,000 men. Their army also included six Panzer (armoured) divisions which had grown to ten by the time of the invasion of France, although most of the tanks were at best only of medium quality. Thus, against the western forces, the Germans did not have any great preponderance. In the east against the Poles they certainly did, since the Polish army consisted of thirty active divisions, of which only one was motorised, and Germany was likely to be successful in any confrontation here, provided that the western Allies did not distract her with a war on two fronts (**22, 34**).

Comparisons of naval strength are always complicated by the question of building programmes, but it is clear that in September 1939 Great Britain still held a substantial lead with ten battleships, three battle cruisers, four aircraft carriers and sixteen cruisers. France also had considerable strength with five battleships, two battle cruisers and ten cruisers. In contrast to this, the German fleet was small – two old battleships, two battle cruisers, three pocket battleships, eight cruisers and only twenty-six U-boats capable of operating in the Atlantic. This reflected Hitler's earlier hope that he could avoid a clash with the western Powers, if he was careful not to embark on a naval race with Great Britain. It was not until the end of 1938 that he allowed plans to be made for a greatly enlarged navy, but the building of this would not have been completed before the end of 1944. Consequently, from the point of view of Admiral Raeder, the German naval commander-in-chief, Hitler's war in 1939 was fatally premature (**5, 28**).

In the air the positions were reversed. In September 1939 the British had 1,460 front line aircraft, of which 536 were bombers and

608 fighters, while the French had 463 bombers and 634 fighters. In contrast, the German air force, the Luftwaffe, had a front line strength of 3,400, including 1,180 bombers, 1,100 fighters and 366 dive-bombers. In addition to this, the French planes were largely obsolescent, and the German bombers were technologically superior to the British; the single-engined Messerschmitt, too, was superior to most British fighters, except for the Spitfire and the Hurricane which were only just coming into mass production (**8, 23**).

As well as these orthodox comparisons, there is also a variety of special weapons to be considered. At the start the Germans already had a magnetic mine which exploded on the seabed when affected by the magnetic field of a ship passing above it. Both the British and the Germans had established the principle of radar, although the British were further advanced in setting up a line of stations along their south and east coasts with a central control system directly connected with the air command. Apparently unknown to the Germans, the British also had Asdic, a kind of underwater radar, which could detect the distance and direction of U-boats, but not their depth.

An important development lay in the invention of an encoding machine called Enigma, which the Germans used throughout the war. The most startling aspect of this was that the Poles had managed to design a replica of it before the war, and by January 1938 were reading most of the German messages. After that, however, the Germans had added two more wheels to their machine and this meant that Poles were left in the dark. Even so, a fortnight before the outbreak of war they did hand over two replicas, one to the British and one to the French, and at the British intelligence centre at Bletchley Park an organisation known as Ultra worked on the new complexities of the Enigma machine until by April 1940 most intercepted radio messages to and from the German high command could be decoded, translated and despatched to the relevant commanders (**16, 17**).

The size and organisation of their forces often revealed the form which the various general staffs imagined any future war would take. In France the main obsession had been defence against Germany, and since 1930, when the Allies had removed their occupation forces from the Rhineland five years ahead of schedule, a highly elaborate fortification, the Maginot Line, had been constructed along the common frontier with Germany. In the event of war the French reckoned simply to man this with a large conscript army and they had no plans for creating an independent striking force.

As far as the British were concerned, an army would be shipped to France and the navy would impose its blockade. The new element was the RAF, whose leaders during the inter-war years had been determined that air power should operate as a weapon in its own right rather than as an auxiliary to the army and the navy. By the same token they had conceived a separate and decisive role for the RAF, whereby Bomber Command would carry out an overwhelming strategic air offensive which would so destroy an enemy country's ability to make war that the only function of the military would be to move in afterwards to occupy the smoking ruins (**6**). As a consequence, during the year before the outbreak of war, the British air staff contemplated a far higher proportion of bombers to fighters, but by September 1939 they still had nothing like the bomber force needed to give expression to their intended strategy.

Neither the French nor the British prognoses proved very accurate. The Maginot Line was outflanked through Belgium in May 1940, and it was not until the last part of 1944 that the strategic air offensive began to achieve its fundamental object (see p. 45). The Germans, on the other hand, had concentrated on the organisation of Panzer armoured divisions, and one school of thought among the professionals had developed the notion of what came to be known as *Blitzkrieg*. By this method an advance guard of armoured columns, supported by dive-bombers, would sweep through to the rear of the enemy's lines, cutting his communications and paralysing his forces amid noise and confusion. This imaginative combination of infantry, armour and aircraft, relying on mobility and surprise, had already been suggested by two military commentators in Great Britain, Major-General Fuller and Captain Liddell Hart, but the British general staff had on the whole preferred to keep tank forces as a separate entity to be distributed piecemeal among infantry units. Thus it is ironical that British theorists should have suggested the very tactics that the Germans applied so successfully in Poland and France, as the major German exponent of them, General Guderian, admitted in his autobiography [**doc. 1a, b**]. It would, however, be wrong to imagine that the German high command had unquestioningly accepted the notion of *Blitzkrieg*. Many of the more conservative were as doubtful as their British counterparts; they wished to keep the armoured divisions with the main body of the army, where they

would participate in encircling manoeuvres with a pincer movement from each flank. Indeed, Guderian was only able to achieve
what he did in France in 1940 by misinterpreting his orders to the
utmost until his success ruled out further argument (**48**).

*Blitzkrieg* belongs to the early years of the war; it could
accomplish little, once the great slogging match had developed
over the plains of Russia. Yet at the time it was a remarkably
successful and economical route to victory for the Germans. This
was made possible by the absence of any similar striking force
among the Allies, which could easily have threatened to cut off the
Panzers so deep in enemy territory. It would be unfair, however,
to blame the Allied commanders in the field for this, since the
means of retaliation could not swiftly be improvised at the height
of the enemy attack and the commanders were largely the victims
of the decisions and preparations made years before the war.

Thus German military expertise had played a large part in their
victories of the first year, and it was on this that Hitler had to rely
when he launched his attack on Russia in June 1941, since the
apparent balance of forces was hardly in his favour. For their
campaign the Germans had over three million men in 148 divisions, including nineteen Panzers, some 3,500 tanks and 7,000
pieces of artillery. Against this, the strength of the Red Army
initially was some 200 divisions – as German Intelligence had
estimated (see p. 75) – as well as 7,000 tanks and a superiority
in the number of artillery pieces. Clearly a great deal would
depend upon the respective quality of the troops, equipment and
leadership.

Hitler's principal hope lay once again in the technique of *Blitzkrieg*, to which the Russians had no immediate answer [**doc. 4**].
Their tanks were scattered up and down the line among various
infantry units and it was only after the beginning of hostilities that
they turned seriously to the grouping of armoured divisions. Their
air force was shattered within the first few days and the plains of
Russia provided an ideal theatre for the onrush of the German
Panzers. Hitler reckoned also that the Soviet regime was ripe for
internal collapse and that Stalin's recent purges had done great
harm to the whole structure of the Russian military machine.
Indeed, the poor performance of the Red Army in the Finnish war
from December 1939 to March 1940 (see p. 8) gave him every
reason to think so. There was a further weakness in the layout of
the Russian defence. Until 1939 this had been concentrated on a
so-called Stalin line which ran intermittently between Pskov and

Odessa, but after the partition of Poland in September 1939 the bulk of the Russian forces had been moved west and were not sufficiently organised or dug in to be able to resist the German assault. All calculation of relative strength, however, became outdated when the Russian army, in spite of its desperate losses, was able to maintain its defence and, once the eastern front had been established, the Soviet Union was eventually to fall back on reserves of war production and manpower that the German staff had utterly under-estimated (**74, 76**).

# Part Two:   The Course of the War on the Land

## 2   The Overrunning of the Continent: September 1939–June 1940

### The Polish campaign: September 1939

Early in the morning of 1 September 1939 two German Army Groups, one in the north under von Bock, the other in the south under von Rundstedt, thrust eastwards into Poland. On 3 September Great Britain and France declared war on Germany in accordance with their treaties with Poland, but for the moment these were the only combatants. Mussolini had already informed Hitler that Italy was not yet ready for war, and the rest of Europe merely watched in the hope of being allowed to remain in a state of neutrality. Only Russia prepared to move west to take her share in the partition of Poland agreed by the Molotov-Ribbentrop pact of 23 August.

The entry of Great Britain and France into the war did little to save the Poles. It was to take several weeks for the British contingents to be shipped across the Channel, and the French were hampered by the complications of mobilising a large conscript army and by the absence of any force organised for immediate attack. Thus, except for a small French diversion on the western front in the middle of September, the Germans were free to concentrate on the assault on Poland.

Before long, the Poles were close to collapse. National sentiment and the location of the Silesian coalfields had caused them to place their forces too far to the west, where they were open to envelopment by the German Third Army striking south from East Prussia at the same time as the two Army Groups attacked eastwards. More particularly, their army was organised on old-fashioned lines and had to face a remarkable German demonstration of *Blitzkrieg*, in which six armoured divisions, four light divisions and four motorised divisions drove on relentlessly, weaving around and behind the slow-moving Polish forces ill-equipped to deal with tanks supported by dive-bombers. By 4 September German tanks were 80 kilometres into Poland, and by 8 September one army corps had reached the outskirts of Warsaw. A German swing northwards cut off much of the Polish army west of the Vistula and the chances of the rest, who were ordered to fall back on south-east Poland, were shattered on 17 September, when Soviet Russia moved into eastern Poland. By the end of the month Poland had been competely occupied (**11**).

## The Scandinavian flank: Finland, Denmark, Norway

After the Polish campaign there was a strange lull, as the western Powers and Germany each contemplated the ways in which they might attack their enemy. During this winter of what was called the phoney war Scandinavia came increasingly to occupy the thoughts of both sides. The western Allies knew that the Germans were drawing on a vital supply of iron ore from north Sweden and transporting it by sea from Narvik through Norwegian territorial waters. The Germans were well aware that the Allies might try to stop this; they were also loath to embark on an assault on France before ensuring that their north coast could not be threatened by an Allied occupation of Norwegian ports.

Thus, throughout these months both sides were considering some form of preventive action in Norway, but in the event, the first major conflict in the Scandinavian world was to break out further east. By the middle of October Russia had consolidated her hold on the eastern half of Poland and had established garrisons in Estonia, Latvia and Lithuania. All this was with an eye to bolstering up her western frontier against an eventual German attack and it was natural that she should now wish to strengthen her position on the north side of the Gulf of Finland. The Finns, however, refused to cede part of the Karelian isthmus, some islands in the Gulf and a lease on a port at the extreme south-western end of Finland, all in exchange for territory further north. Consequently, on 30 November 1939 the winter war opened with an attack by the Russians on the Karelian isthmus, where a remarkable resistance by the Finns in the Mannerheim line held them off until March 1940, when Russia's terms had to be accepted.

The poor performance of the Red Army certainly encouraged Hitler to make his attack on Russia a year later. The immediate consequence of the Finnish war, however, was to provide the west with a pretext for sending out an expeditionary force to north

Norway, nominally on their way to aid the Finns, but in fact to capture the Swedish ore mines. This force was almost ready to sail when Finland surrendered, but Hitler, convinced that the west was going to take Norway, decided to strike first. On 9 April 1940 Denmark offered no resistance to a German occupation, and sea-borne German forces captured the principal ports along the Norwegian coast. British and French forces were rushed across to attempt to regain the centre and north of Norway, but before the end of May the whole of Norway had been lost to Germany, and in London the anger of members of the House of Commons resulted in the fall of Neville Chamberlain, who was replaced by Winston Churchill at the head of a coalition government (**40**).

## The Battle of France: May–June 1940

Meanwhile, throughout the winter the British Expeditionary Force (BEF) in France had been built up to ten divisions under the command of Lord Gort. The French army under General Gamelin numbered ninety-four divisions, many of which manned the Maginot Line, while the rest worked with the British in preparing defensive positions along the Franco-Belgian border north of the point where the Maginot Line ended.

As it turned out, these positions were hardly to be used. On 10 May, the very day when Winston Churchill became Prime Minister in Great Britain, the Germans launched their western assault through the Low Countries (see Map A, p. 10). To secure their right wing, the Netherlands were attacked with an airborne landing at Rotterdam, which was soon reinforced by armour breaking through from the south. At the same time other airborne forces had captured a Belgian frontier fortress as well as the bridges over the Belgian canals, to allow an Army Group under General von Bock to thrust into Belgium from the east. On this violation of Belgian neutrality the whole of the British Expeditionary Force and a part of the French army advanced into Belgium to form a combined line of defence along the Scheldt estuary and the river Dyle to the east of Brussels (**35**).

In fact, the attack by von Bock's Army Group did not represent the main thrust of the German advance. This was to come further south from von Rundstedt's Army Group, within which three Panzer corps were to strike through Luxemburg and to make for the Meuse. The French had considered the Ardennes difficult terrain for tanks and had left the area lightly guarded. They also

## A   May – June 1940

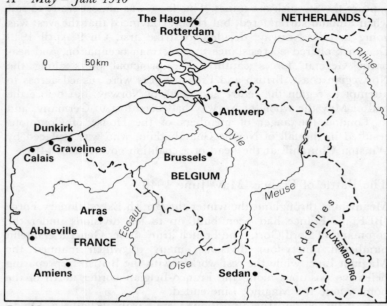

## B   Normandy, June – August 1944

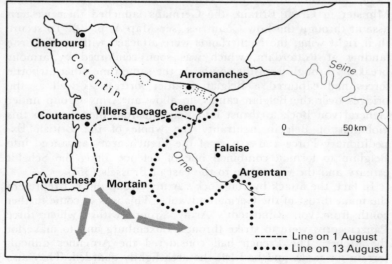

reckoned that the Germans would need several days to prepare for the crossing of the Meuse, after they had reached it, but in this they underestimated the quality of German staff work and the philosophy of *Blitzkrieg*. By 13 May General Guderian, commanding the leading armoured formations, was already at the Meuse, and crossed it on the same day to the west of Sedan with the aid of dive-bombers. Stretching his orders to the limit, he now pressed on to the Oise, and by 20 May he had reached the Channel at Abbeville (**48**). Thus, the opposing forces were rotating like a revolving door; in the north the Allies pushed east to the aid of the Belgians, while in the south a great tank drive westwards by the Germans had cut the Allied line in half and sealed off the northern part against the Channel (**68, 70**).

Nevertheless, the German high command remained nervous, lest the Allies should produce the obvious counter-stroke – an attack from north and south on the sides of the corridor created by the German armoured thrust. They were to be spared this, mainly because the Allies in their pre-war military thinking had never attempted the creation of an armoured striking force which might well have halted the German operation. Amid the confusion which was one of the main elements of *Blitzkrieg*, Gamelin was busy preparing such a counter-attack, but on 19 May he was sacked and replaced by General Weygand who cancelled the plan and then, after a three days' delay, produced a very similar one (**46**).

Gort had already attempted a southward push at Arras, but this had petered out, and on the evening of 25 May, conscious that his east flank could easily collapse, he took a decision on his own initiative to pull back to Dunkirk. On the next day the British cabinet confirmed this decision; on 27 May the Belgian government finally surrendered, thus leaving Gort's east flank wide open, and there ensued a desperate race for the sea. The navy had already been ordered to make preparations for a major evacuation and by 2 June 224,000 British troops and 95,000 French had been successfully extricated, before the dwindling bridgehead around Dunkirk finally succumbed, as von Bock pushed in from the east and the Panzers from the west (**35**).

By now the main part of the French army had fallen back on the Somme and the Aisne, and a new German offensive launched on 5 June had reached the Seine by 7 June and crossed the Marne on 11 June. At this point Italy declared war on France, although her attack in the south was held. On that day the French Premier, Reynaud, resigned, and his successor, Marshal Pétain, asked for

11

an armistice which took France out of the war and left Hitler in control of the Continent from the Pyrenees to eastern Poland.

Chance had affected the German assault through the Low Countries into France. Until January 1940 the plan for this attack had been based on a thrust through Belgium by the extreme northern wing of the German army, aiming at the junction point of the British and French armies and hoping to break through to the Channel ports. In fact, this was exactly the tactic that the French commander General Gamelin had been expecting and he had disposed his forces accordingly. Thus, if the attack had come in this way, it is possible that it might have been held, and with the development of an enduring front in the west the whole pattern of the war would have been different. Had it lasted into 1941, for example, it is extremely improbable that Hitler would have launched an attack on Russia.

However, this first plan for a German offensive had to be abandoned after papers outlining a part of it were captured on 10 January 1940, when a staff officer flying to Cologne had gone off course and made a forced landing in Belgium. The need for a different plan provided an opportunity to put forward one which had been suggested by General von Manstein and had already attracted Hitler's attention. By February 1940 the design had taken shape for the main thrust to be made further south through the Ardennes, over the Meuse and then turning north to the Channel ports. This new plan, far more imaginative than the original one, was to be the basis of the German defeat of France that summer.

Speculation on the chances of breaking the corridor that cut the Allies in two must remain as confused as the scene of the battle itself. The lack of any Allied strategic reserve and the disconcerting impact of *Blitzkrieg* with the use of armour and tactical air power seem to make it unlikely, but with stronger leadership and morale in France and Belgium and with different forms of preparation during the pre-war years it might have been possible; as it was, the French armies to the south were driven back to defeat and surrender.

The continuation of the war beyond the summer of 1940 now depended upon the British attitude and this can be seen to rest on four decisions. Three of these affected the material ability of Great Britain to carry on alone. The first was taken by Lord Gort on 25 May (see p. 11), when he desisted on his own responsibility from any further attempt to break out to the south and pulled back two divisions to plug a dangerous gap on his left flank, preparatory to moving towards the coast. Within two days the Belgian surrender had created an even greater gap on his left, and this would suggest that he had acted only just in time. Thus his decision probably gave the BEF its only chance of survival that summer, although this could still not be rated very highly at the moment when it was taken. Indeed, if the Belgian surrender had come a couple of days earlier, as it could well have done, there would probably have been no chance of survival at all.

Gort's successful withdrawal within a perimeter around Dunkirk, however, was also made possible by a second decision, this time by the Germans, when they halted their armoured attack on 24 May, as it was pushing eastwards from Gravelines towards Dunkirk (**48**). There has been endless debate over the responsibility for the order. At first, the German generals blamed Hitler; then it seemed that von Rundstedt had advised it and Hitler had merely agreed. There is debate also over the reasons – practical, in that the armies needed a rest to consolidate before moving on to ground that might be less suitable for tanks; and political, in that Hitler did not wish to crush the British, if they were to be persuaded to make peace – although this hardly tallies with the orders given to the Luftwaffe over the beaches. Probably at the end the responsibility has to be shared and the motive was no more than excessive caution, perhaps encouraged by Gort's short-lived counter-attack at Arras (see p. 11). At any rate, by the time the armoured advance had started again on 26 May, Gort had the BEF and a part of the French First Army within the Dunkirk perimeter. The evacuation there eventually saved enough British troops to form the nucleus of a new army, and but for that a continuation of the war would hardly have been feasible. To this one must add the chance of a calm sea – without which no decision-making would have been of much significance.

There remains the question of aircraft. Churchill had had to face constant demands from the French for all the Hurricane fighters in Great Britain to be dispatched to France, but on 15 May Air Chief Marshal Dowding had been able to persuade him that no more could be sent, if there was to be any hope for the later defence of the United Kingdom. In fact, additional squadrons were sent, although many operated from bases in Great Britain, and, in all, the RAF lost 931 planes in the Battle of France, including 477 fighters (**8**).

Nevertheless, the residue of air power, plus the troops rescued from Dunkirk, made possible the fourth decision – one taken almost imperceptibly. On 22 June the French signed the armistice at Réthondes, and on 19 July in a speech to the Reichstag Hitler made a somewhat contemptuous offer of peace to the British. Already at the end of May Churchill had made it clear that under his government there would be no surrender, and this policy had been supported by a fairly cool assessment by the chiefs of staff [**doc. 2a**].

# 3   The Uncertain Options: June 1940–June 1941

## The Battle of Britain: August–September 1940

After Dunkirk Hitler had been principally concerned with the defeat of France. Once that had been accomplished, he reckoned that it would not be long before the British came to terms, and it was only after Churchill's government had put this out of the question that Hitler turned seriously to considering the prospects for an invasion, and that the plans for Operation Sea-Lion began to develop (**69**).

Even so, he was not entirely single-minded over this, since he was already speaking of an invasion of Russia for 1941. There was, too, a growing awareness of the difficulty of invading Great Britain. It meant the accumulation of masses of landing craft, and the intercepted signals decoded at Bletchley showed that all western Europe was being scoured for barges. The army contemplated a bridgehead between Brighton and Folkestone, with ten divisions landing in two days, after which there would be an expansion in a roughly north-westerly direction. In order to achieve this, they needed a broad corridor for the crossing of the Channel, whereas the German navy could only guarantee a narrow one. In any case, as both the British and German chiefs of staff realised, neither a broad nor a narrow corridor would be possible, unless the German Luftwaffe could gain air superiority around it [**doc. 2a, b**].

All these problems made it clear to Hitler that there could be no invasion before the middle of September, but in the meantime Goering was keen to win a great victory over the RAF, and since this was the vital preliminary, Hitler agreed to let him go ahead. For the battle which raged throughout August Goering could call on two air fleets with a combined strength of 875 bombers, 316 dive-bombers and 929 fighters. Against this Air Chief Marshal Dowding at the head of Fighter Command had some 650 fighters by the middle of July, after having already lost nearly 500 in France. Supply was likely to increase, after Lord Beaverbrook had taken over as Minister of Aircraft Production, but pilots would be more difficult to replace and Dowding had to be careful to avoid being drawn into a battle of attrition which he knew he could not win.

In July the main target for German bombers had been shipping in the Channel, but at the beginning of August this was switched to the airfields and radar stations in the south-east of England in the hope of drawing the bulk of the RAF into conflict. Dependent on information from observer corps posts, radar and intercepted enemy orders decoded at Bletchley, Dowding carefully husbanded his resources and kept enough squadrons in the north to beat off the diversionary attack from German bases in Norway. The battle reached its final climax on 15 August with a German attack of 500 bombers, of which they lost seventy-five, in comparison with British losses of thirty-five fighters. After this Goering shifted the brunt of his attack further inland and by the beginning of September the comparative losses on each side suggested that the Germans now only had to persevere. Their own replacement of losses, however, was beginning to break down; morale, too, had been affected by the continuing resistance of the RAF, and on 7 September Goering made his final fatal switch of target to London itself, carrying out an immense raid on the docks with a thousand planes. For subsequent months London was to soak up the destructive energies of the Luftwaffe, particularly in an all-out attack on 15 September, but for the British this meant salvation, as the attack on the airfields and radar stations lifted (**8**).

Throughout the entire battle up to the end of October the Germans lost 1,733 planes, the British 915, but before that the shift to the attack on London had been a tacit acknowledgement by the Germans that the British still controlled their own air space. This meant that invasion was impossible; in addition, the weather was growing rougher with the equinoctial gales, and the logistical requirements for the Germans had still not been met (**33**). Consequently, in October Hitler postponed any further attempt until the spring of 1941, by which time he had decided to push eastwards, even though he had not yet closed down the war in the west.

## Changes of fortune along the North African coast

Throughout the winter the German bombing of London and of large provincial cities continued. The British carried on their own bombing of targets in Germany, consolidated their naval blockade, and in July 1940, when French battleships in North African ports refused to surrender, sank or disabled them, in case the government of unoccupied France at Vichy should hand them over to Hitler. Ties with the United States were strengthened by a personal correspondence between Churchill and the American President Roosevelt. Apart from this, however, Great Britain and Germany lacked for the moment any area where they could come to grips.

The only theatre of land operations was provided by Mussolini, since Italy's declaration of war on France in June 1940 had finally committed her to the side of Germany. The Italians had established vast forces in their African empire – 200,000 men in Abyssinia and Eritrea against 9,000 British in the Sudan, and even more Italians in Cyrenaica (Libya) against 36,000 British in Egypt. In these circumstances it was not surprising that Mussolini should decide on an advance into Egypt (see map on p. 18). By September, however, Marshal Graziani's forces had got no further than Sidi Barrani and the British commander-in-chief, General Wavell, decided to give his enemy a jolt. The outcome was a remarkable testimony to the doctrine of *Blitzkrieg* and the imaginative deployment of mobile armoured forces. Between December 1940 and February 1941 General O'Connor used the small number of tanks at his disposal for a series of left-flanking movements out into the desert and then into the rear of the Italians. Within weeks he had advanced 800 kilometres, was south of Benghazi and had captured thousands of prisoners. At the same time thrusts from the Sudan and Kenya had mopped up Italian forces in Abyssinia and Eritrea, and in May 1941 the exiled Emperor of Abyssinia re-entered his capital of Addis Ababa. Meanwhile, at sea the British had carried out a successful air attack on Italian battleships at Taranto in November 1940 and had had a victorious engagement with their fleet off Cape Matapan in March 1941.

The success on the north coast of Africa was not to last. Early in February 1941 the advance from Benghazi was stopped on orders from Churchill, so that forces could be withdrawn and be sent to Greece, now threatened by Hitler. And at almost exactly the same time the German General Rommel arrived in Tripoli, from where he launched a series of lightning attacks, when the British were in the middle of their reorganisaton. As a consequence, they were soon driven into retreat. O'Connor himself was captured and by the middle of their reorganisation. As a consequence, they were **71**).

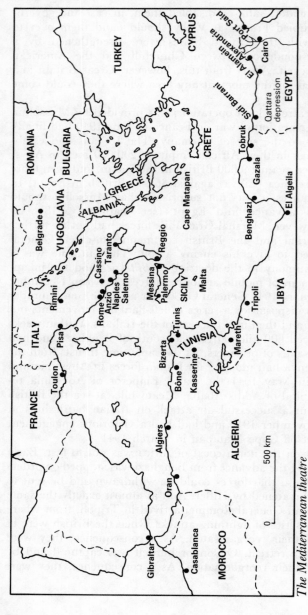

*The Mediterranean theatre*

## The Balkan flank: Yugoslavia, Greece, Crete

Mussolini had already opened his own offensive against Greece from Albania at the end of October 1940. From a political point of view it would be an important gesture for the British to stand firm by yet another victim of Axis aggression, and the diverting of troops from the desert could well have begun at any time after that. The Greeks, however, who reckoned that they could manage the Italians, were not at first very keen to receive help; they only finally agreed in February 1941, and on 7 March a British contingent of 50,000 began to land in Greece.

Hitler himself had never much cared for Mussolini's venture. It might tempt the British to take advantage of the situation, and in any case he was not keen that Italy should strengthen her position in the Balkans, although the lack of Italian success in the fighting must soon have allayed that fear. Before long, however, Hitler's determination to attack Russia created a separate German interest in the Balkans, since he knew that he must first secure his right flank there before embarking on the principal campaign.

Mostly he hoped to work politically. Romania was won over to his side, after the Russians had seized Bessarabia and northern Bukovina from her in June 1940. On 1 March 1941 Bulgaria also agreed to allow German forces in. A similar agreement was signed with the Yugoslavs on 25 March, but a military coup carried out two days later in Belgrade set up a new government which rejected this agreement.

Hitler now decided that he must settle at once with Yugoslavia and Greece. On 1 April the invasion of Russia was postponed until 22 June, and on 6 April German forces broke into Yugoslavia from Austria, Hungary and Bulgaria, and thence into Greece. By 17 April the fighting in Yugoslavia was over and by 21 April in Greece, where those of the British forces who could be saved were evacuated to Crete. Here on 20 May they were followed by a German airborne landing under General Student who, despite the information that the British had received through Ultra, achieved a surprise, and with the capture of one airfield was eventually able to land 22,000 troops. By 28 May the British had been forced to give up the island to the Germans and Hitler was now free to turn his mind back to Russia.

# 4 The Turning Points: June 1941–November 1942

In the second half of 1941 there took place two major extensions of the conflict that brought Great Britain out of her state of isolation. In June 1941 Hitler launched his invasion of Russia, and Churchill at once proclaimed an alliance with the Soviet Union, making immediate arrangements for the despatch of supplies by sea to Murmansk. Then, in December 1941, Japan opened her assault on the United States by attacking the American Navy in Hawaii, and when Germany also declared war in support of Japan, the two blocs of the war had finally emerged; the United States, Great Britain and Russia now confronted Germany, Italy and Japan, and the scales had tipped decisively to Hitler's disadvantage.

## Hitler's attack on Russia:.summer 1941

On 22 June 1941 three German Army Groups began Hitler's offensive against Russia (**74**). In the north Leeb was to strike through the Baltic states towards Leningrad; in the centre von Bock along the line Minsk-Smolensk towards Moscow; and in the south Rundstedt into the Ukraine [**doc. 4**]. Of the three von Bock had the major role, for which he had been given two of the four available Panzer groups. These, however, were not to be used in an independent thrust, as in France in 1940, and as Guderian would have liked. Hitler insisted that the prime object was not the acquisition of territory or of cities, but the destruction of the Red Army, which was to be accomplished by double pincer operations of infantry and armour moving round on the left and right flanks of Russian units. The whole campaign was designed to be swift and short, and Hitler reckoned to be in Moscow before the onset of winter.

Two factors upset this plan: first, the extraordinary stubbornness of the Russian resistance, even when many of their forces had been encircled, with the result that the pincer failed to close in time to capture the bulk of them; and second, summer rain that turned the roads into swamps and immobilised wheeled transport [**doc. 5**].

*The Russian front, 1941–44*

Thus, by the beginning of August, the German army had been drawn in as far east as Smolensk in pursuit of an elusive foe. At this point Hitler, concerned about the economic potential of the Ukraine, switched his effort to the south [**doc. 6**]. Here an encircling operation east of Kiev did have some success, but when at the end of September the thrust towards Moscow was taken up again by the centre group, winter was approaching and by the beginning of December 1941 the German advance had ground to a halt in the snow on the outskirts of Moscow.

Thus, although the Russians had lost over two and a quarter million square kilometres of their European territory, as well as four million dead and three and a half million prisoners, the Red

21

Army with its vast potential for mobilisation was still in the field against the Germans, whom Hitler in his optimism had sent into battle without any winter equipment. In December the Red Army launched its own counter-offensive and only Hitler's indomitable will prevented a general retreat. Throughout the winter the Russian advance pushed back 240 kilometres in places, but it could only wash around the strongpoints that their enemy still held and eventually in May 1942 the Germans were ready for their second offensive.

## Pearl Harbour and the entry of the United States into the war: December 1941

At the same time as the German offensive came to a halt outside Moscow, the Japanese transformed the scene of the war by an action of their own. Since 1895 they had been seeking intermittently to increase their power in China and the Pacific, and this policy was bound sooner or later to bring them into conflict with the United States. The climax came in July 1941, when Japan took advantage of France's recent defeat to establish control over French Indo-China, and in retaliation the United States, with the support of the British and the Dutch, proclaimed a trade embargo on Japan.

The Japanese response to this came on 7 December 1941, when they launched an air attack from aircraft carriers against the American naval base at Pearl Harbour on Hawaii. The surge of conquest by Japan that followed was spectacular – Hong Kong in December, Malaya early in 1942, Singapore in February, the Philippines and Burma in April, as well as the sinking of a British battleship, the *Prince of Wales*, and a battle cruiser *Repulse*.

Two political consequences of Pearl Harbour, however, were to diminish the long-term effect of this. First, Hitler decided to throw in his lot with the Japanese (see p. 77) and declared war on the United States on 11 December. Second, Winston Churchill, seizing his chance at once, was in Washington by Christmas and although there was to be much debate over the nature of later Anglo-American operations (see p. 59), a positive decision was taken that the defeat of Germany was to have priority over that of Japan [**doc. 7a, b**]. Since the outbreak of war Roosevelt, always in close touch with Churchill, had been edging his country towards supporting the British – with Lend-Lease in 1941 and an extension of the patrolling of the Atlantic (see p. 48) – and now Hitler had provided the means whereby they could openly stand together against him.

## The military turning points: October–November 1942

Provided that it could hold together, the Grand Alliance of the United States, Great Britain and Russia certainly made Hitler's defeat more likely. It did not immediately check the advance of the Axis Powers. By the autumn of 1942 they were as far east as the Caucasus, and on the African coast Rommel stood within easy reach of Cairo and the Suez canal – all foreshadowing an immense German pincer, meeting in the Middle East. This, however, was the peak of their strength and they were now about to suffer three decisive defeats – two in North Africa and one at Stalingrad in Russia.

(A) NORTH AFRICA AND THE BATTLE OF EL ALAMEIN: OCTOBER 1942

It has been seen (p. 17) how by April 1941 British forces had been pushed back to the Egyptian frontier (**73**). All that was left to them further west was the port of Tobruk, which Rommel made two efforts to capture in April, but without success. This was followed in May and June by two attempts by Wavell to push Rommel back. After the second of these had failed, Wavell was replaced by General Auchinleck, who until August 1942 continued to fight a swift-moving duel with Rommel in the desert (see map on p. 18).

Both generals had their problems of supply. The bulk of Auchinleck's supplies had to come round the Cape, although in May 1941 Churchill had taken the desperate risk of ordering one convoy through the Mediterranean to run the gauntlet of Axis air power, and four out of five ships had reached Alexandria to deliver 238 tanks to the British forces. Rommel's supplies came directly across the Mediterranean, so harassed by attack from Malta, where the command was well informed of his convoys' sailings by Bletchley (see p. 50), that in April 1942 Hitler briefly contemplated a landing on the island. However, the heavy cost of a similar landing in Crete the previous year, together with his mistrust of the Italians, combined to persuade him to abandon the idea [**doc. 8**].

The duel began in November 1941 with an offensive named 'Crusader' undertaken by the British Eighth Army, and during a long fluctuating battle Rommel counter-attacked with an armoured thrust behind British lines and then eventually fell back to a position just west of Agheila. From here he launched a new offensive in January 1942, which caused the British to retreat to Gazala, and a second in May developed into a confused and fluid battle, in which Tobruk fell to Rommel, and the British drew back as far as El Alamein, only 240 kilometres west of Cairo. In July, however, Rommel was unable to break through the line which they had established there, and the armies settled down to confront each other in a position where the Qattara depression of quicksand to the south prevented any outflanking movement (**67, 71**).

In August 1942 Churchill, on his way to Moscow, flew to Cairo and replaced Auchinleck with General Sir Harold Alexander as commander-in-chief, while General Sir Bernard Montgomery took over command of the Eighth Army. At the end of the month Rommel made a further attempt to break through the southern half of the line and then to wheel north, but this had been anticipated by Auchinleck and his staff before their departure and had in any case been confirmed by a decoded message from Bletchley, with the result that the battle of Alam Halfa was a positive rebuff for Rommel (**39**).

Montgomery's own offensive was launched on 23 October with an old-style frontal attack preceded by an immense bombardment, but it was to take three separate planned assaults over the next twelve days to create the gap in Rommel's defence through which the armoured divisions could break out. This second battle of El Alamein finally brought the to and fro in the desert to an end, and this time, as the British continued their pursuit of Rommel westwards, there was to be no return.

(B) OPERATION TORCH: THE LANDINGS IN MOROCCO AND
ALGERIA: NOVEMBER 1942
The principal reason why the German retreat was not to stop was that on 8 November 1942 the Allies made three landings at the extreme western end of the North African coast, all under the supreme command of the American General Eisenhower – at Casablanca with an American force sailing straight from Virginia, at Oran with an American force from the Clyde, and at Algiers with a mixed British and American force. Immediate resistance to Operation Torch could have come from 120,000 French troops in Algeria, under the command of Pétain's Vichy government, and the operation had been preceded by careful soundings of the local authorities – undertaken partly by an American General Mark

Clark, who was landed clandestinely from a British submarine not far from Algiers.

These preparations were not totally successful in preventing an initial resistance, but the Allies were fortunate in that Admiral Darlan, Pétain's second-in-command, who happened to be in Algiers, was prepared to offer a cautious collaboration, and acceptance of the Allies' presence became outright after a suspicious Hitler ordered the occupation of Vichy France on 10 November. The French fleet at Toulon was the remaining danger, but to Anglo-American relief this scuttled itself on the approach of the Germans. Darlan was now made High Commissioner, but at Christmas his assassination by a young Frenchman relieved the Allies of a somewhat embarrassing associate and his place was taken by General Giraud.

Algeria was now secured and Rommel was consequently caught between two fires. Yet the Allied failure to make their landings sufficiently far to the east meant that they had not gained control of Tunisia, where Hitler immediately began pumping in troops who were to make sure that the African campaign ran on well into 1943.

(C) STALINGRAD: NOVEMBER 1942

Meanwhile, in May 1942 Hitler had launched his second Russian offensive, although by then many of the senior German commanders had been removed, mostly at their own request. The main direction of the new attack was to be a thrust through the south into the Caucasus, accompanied by an advance on its left flank to take Stalingrad on the Volga (see map on p. 21).

Early in July the Crimea, including Sebastopol, had been overrun and by the end of the month a front had been established along the lower waters of the Don; by the middle of August the Germans were deep into the Caucasus, but throughout the next six weeks they were unable quite to reach the shore of the Caspian or the eastern end of the Black Sea. At the same time the Russian resistance around Stalingrad had so infuriated Hitler that, in his determination to capture it, he eventually began to divert troops away from his primary objective in the Caucasus [**doc. 10**] and also to weaken his defences along the 640 kilometres of his northern flank between Voronezh and Stalingrad (**76**).

It was here to the east and west of Stalingrad that the first pincer movements of the Russian counter-offensive were launched on 19 November 1942. The German Sixth Army under General Paulus, fighting in the ruins of Stalingrad, was cut off; a second wider pincer movement now captured the routes along which he might have been relieved, and on 16 December a third still wider movement gained control of most of the land between the Don and the Donetz. The extent of this Russian victory naturally threatened the German forces further south in the Caucasus and in January 1943 Hitler agreed to their withdrawal westwards, shortly before Paulus finally surrendered at Stalingrad. It was the beginning of the German retreat, which was only to end when the Russians entered Berlin in May 1945.

# 5 The Long Axis Retreat in Russia and the Mediterranean Area: November 1942–June 1944

## The Russian advance after Stalingrad

By the end of January 1943 von Kleist, who was made a Field Marshal for his efforts, had succeeded in extricating the German forces westwards through the Crimea and Rostov, before General Rokossovski was able to cut them off with a thrust southwards. The Russians now followed up their victory with offensives in the north. Leningrad, still under siege, was relieved and further south there was a great advance towards Kharkov. By 7 February Kursk had been captured and this created a great westward bulge, which became more pronounced, when, in March, a German counter-offensive pushed the line back to recapture Kharkov to the south of it (see map on p. 21).

The shape of the front had convinced Hitler that the points of attack for his summer offensive must be the sides of the Kursk salient – Operation *Zitadelle* – with Model commanding in the north and Manstein in the south. For this the Germans concentrated almost all the armour at their disposal and on 5 July 1943 the attack opened with the advance of some 2,000 tanks. The Russians, however, had anticipated this and had decided to ward it off before launching their own offensive. Accordingly, they had created a series of defended belts of mines, tanks and anti-tank guns, and after seven days of destructive slogging the Germans withdrew from what one writer has called the greatest tank battle in history (**74**).

For the rest of that summer attack upon attack by the Russians drove the line steadily towards the south-west. The war had revealed the talents of a younger generation of generals who exploited the sheer space on the Russian front in launching a series of separate thrusts from different parts of the line; supplies of food, medical equipment and half-track vehicles from Great Britain and the United States meant that the Russian war industry could concentrate on tanks and guns, which soon outnumbered the

German armament; and their soldiers seemed to be able to fight and advance on a diet that no western soldier could have endured. And all the time Hitler's refusal to countenance limited withdrawal forced his generals to continue to fight in unfavourable conditions.

By the end of September 1943 the Russians under Koniev were past Kiev and Kharkov and had taken Smolensk. By November they had reached the Dnieper and Romanian territory, and by 13 May the Crimea had been overrun and Sebastopol had fallen. In the north the advance had not been so extensive, but by the time the western Allies launched their own invasion of Normandy in June 1944, the Russians were ready for a new offensive which was to mean the destruction of the German Army Group Centre.

## Africa, Sicily and Italy

Very shortly after the landings in Algeria in November 1942, a combined British and American force pushed eastwards with the intention of preventing the Germans gaining control of Bizerta and Tunis. However, a relatively small number of German troops kept them at bay until General von Arnim arrived to organise a defensive position around both towns, from which an Allied offensive just before Christmas failed to dislodge them (see map on p. 18).

Meanwhile, since his victory at El Alamein, Montgomery's Eighth Army had been pursuing Rommel steadily westwards. Twice along the North African coast the German army slipped out of his grasp, until by the end of January 1943 Montgomery had gained the port of Tripoli, while Rommel now occupied the Mareth line on the south Tunisian border. Thus the Allied failure to capture Tunisia at once and Rommel's successful retreat along the coast, together ensured that the African campaign would drift on into 1943.

Rommel's plan for the Axis forces in Tunisia was first to strike out westwards, after which he would turn south against Montgomery at Mareth. The westward attack on 14 February 1943 was initially a success, but slowness in exploiting this enabled the Allies to check the German advance, although the Americans suffered serious casualties at Kasserine Pass. A second German offensive to the north on 25 February was also held and by this time Rommel had to switch his forces back to Mareth.

Here on 6 March he launched a spoiling offensive against Montgomery, who had been informed of Rommel's entire plan through Bletchley and could therefore check it fairly easily. Montgomery's own attack on 20 March was to take seven days to break through, with a frontal assault on the right and a wide flanking movement on the left. The Germans continued to conduct a skilful fighting retreat into the north-east corner of Tunisia, but by the second week of May the Allied command of the sea and air deprived their enemy of food and ammunition and made a German surrender inescapable. At the beginning of February the total Axis force had amounted to 100,000 troops and 280 tanks, but since then, with his usual determination not to yield an inch, Hitler had continued to pour in reinforcements, despite the fact that they were almost certain to be lost. Thus, when the operation finally came to a close in May 1943, the Allies had taken about 150,000 prisoners.

In January 1943 Roosevelt and Churchill in conference at Casablanca had agreed that the next step should be an invasion of Sicily [**doc. 11**] and on 10 July Allied forces landed on either side of the southernmost tip of the island. Here the direct advance of the British Eighth Army from the south was blocked by German Panzers, but General Patton's Second US Army carried out a great left-flanking movement which took Palermo and reached Messina on 17 August.

It was not until 3 September 1943 that Montgomery crossed the Straits of Messina, after which General Mark Clark landed an Anglo-American army at Salerno on 8 September. One reason for this delay was that on 25 July Mussolini had fallen from power (**59**) and the new Italian government had been in secret negotiation with the Allies over a projected change of sides. Hitler, however, had guessed this and immediately after the landings Field Marshal Kesselring was able to disarm and disperse much of the Italian army [**doc. 13**].

The Allies only succeeded in reaching Naples by 1 October, after which Kesselring settled down to holding the so-called Gustav line along the Garigliano river, from where the Allies had not shifted him by the end of the year. In January 1944 they made a new landing at Anzio, just to the south of Rome, which was supposed to link up with a breakthrough at the west end of the Gustav line. The Anzio landing, however, became sealed off and it was to take four major offensives on Monte Cassino, including the bombing of the monastery, to achieve that breakthrough on 17 May. Finally, General Alexander reached Rome on 4 June, but before long the Germans had established a new position, the Gothic line, running roughly between Pisa and Rimini, from which they could continue to delay the Allied advance throughout the rest of 1944.

# 6 The Normandy Invasion and War on Two Fronts: June 1944–May 1945

On 5 June General Eisenhower gave the word for the launching of the Anglo-American Allies' long-awaited cross-Channel invasion, and General Montgomery assumed operational command of all land forces for the campaign. The objective was that part of the Normandy coast held by the German Seventh Army (see Map B, p. 10). In the night two airborne landings had staked a claim to the shoulders of the intended bridgehead, the British Sixth Airborne capturing Pegasus bridge over the canal by the Orne in the east, and the Americans making a fairly scattered drop at the foot of the Cotentin peninsula in the west. Early that morning, on 6 June, more than 4,000 landing craft put down the assault troops of six infantry divisions on five separate beachheads – three British and Canadian in the east, two American in the west – where they fought their way ashore, aided by an extraordinary range of technical devices, such as swimming tanks and mine-blowing flail tanks, and an overwhelming naval and aerial bombardment (**15, 81, 82**).

There has always been an element of glamour in the memory of the Normandy invasion. The sheer magnitude of operation, the thought of two million men locked in battle in July and August 1944, and the spectacular extent of Montgomery's victory, followed by the liberation of France and Belgium, have all given it a place unique in the history of the war. Indeed, one writer maintains that the Normandy campaign was a greater victory in terms of the destruction of enemy units than any comparable action on the Russian front (**83**). This, together with the subsequent end of the war in May 1945, has also encouraged an impression that the Allied success was a foregone conclusion, almost an inescapable epilogue to the story of Hitler's downfall.

It is consequently salutary to recognise that although it was by now clear that Hitler could not win the war, the Germans still had vast forces in the field which might well have warded off total disaster. On 6 June 1944 there were 157 divisions on the eastern front, eleven in Norway and twenty-five in Yugoslavia. The presence of another twenty-five in Italy was a testimony to Brooke's Mediterranean strategy, but that still left fifty-nine in France, ten of which were Panzers, and any concentration of these should very quickly have outnumbered the reinforcements that the Allies had constantly to bring in from the sea.

One element might have wrecked the chances of the invasion, even before it started. Throughout the war there had been considerable German research into pilotless aircraft ('flying bombs') and rockets, and Hitler had been hoping to launch a major bombardment of London and of the southern regions of England by January 1944 (see p. 52). Had he been able to do so, the effect on the invasion plans could have been devastating, since by the early summer of 1944 the whole of the south was crammed with troops, tanks and guns – targets that could not have been missed in the most haphazard inundation of flying bombs. British scientific intelligence, however, had been watching these developments since 1943, and as a result of attacks on factories and launching sites, considerable delays had been imposed on production (**18**). Thus the first pilotless aircraft, the V1, did not land until 13 June, after which the attacks were mostly aimed at London.

Another factor of immense uncertainty was the weather. This caused one twenty-four hour postponement of the landings, and if there had been another, it would have meant waiting a further two weeks for the tide and the moon to be right. On the slender but reasonable hope of a break in the weather, Eisenhower took the chance of going ahead for 6 June and the luck held. Yet thirteen days after the invasion a violent storm lasting three days played havoc with the floating Mulberry harbour and the landing of supplies and reinforcements, and if this had happened earlier and lasted longer, the consequences could have been disastrous.

The most obvious danger was that the Germans might simply drive the invader back into the sea through sheer weight of numbers and armour. The Allies had two ways of countering this. First, they devised an elaborate deception plan, whereby it appeared that the Normandy landing was merely a preliminary feint and that their main thrust was to come further east in the Pas de Calais region. This was so successful that Hitler, who had at first correctly anticipated that the Allies would land in Normandy, insisted long after the invasion had started that the whole of his Fifteenth Army, which lay mostly east of the Seine, should remain there in order to meet the real invasion, when it came. Second, the use of their total supremacy in the air (see p. 44) enabled the Allies to smash the railways and bridges and to dominate the roads along which German divisions in reserve would try to reach the battle area.

It was this Allied air power which lay at the heart of the controversy among German generals over the best way of dealing with the invasion. Von Rundstedt, commander-in-chief west, favoured the orthodox tactics of allowing the invasion area to identify itself, while keeping a large force in reserve at a distance, which could then attack the enemy, once his dispositions had become clear. Rommel, who commanded the armies of northern France, believed that Allied air power was so great that it would be impossible for sufficient reserves to be moved from very far. Hence the reserves must be close at hand and be used to smash the invaders on the beaches, when they would be at their weakest. 'If we are not at the throat of the enemy immediately he lands,' he said, 'there will be no restoring the situation in view of his vastly superior air forces. If we are not able to repulse the Allies at sea or throw them off the mainland in the first forty-eight hours, then the invasion will have succeeded and the war is lost for lack of a strategic reserve and naval and Luftwaffe support' (**50, 52**). Hitler entirely agreed with this method and in the last months before the invasion Rommel was able greatly to improve the beach defences of northern France. Yet he still could not get what he needed as an essential part of his plan – a reserve of some twelve armoured and motorised divisions under his own command, to be stationed not too far away. Hitler, deluded by the deception plan, was determined to keep these under the command of supreme headquarters and at some distance to the east of Paris.

In the event Rommel would seem to have been right, and if he had had more time and been given control of a larger reserve, the Allies might have been driven back into the sea. In the western sector the American airborne division was scattered over far too wide an area and there was heavy fighting on Omaha beach. At the eastern end the British invasion forces were extremely vulnerable throughout the first day; an exceptionally high tide made it difficult to get the tanks off the beaches and thus the two brigades ashore were deprived of much of their armour; a heavy blow struck here with several divisions from the reserve that Rommel had wanted might easily have rolled up the invasion area, although it is impossible to know whether this could eventually have been checked by air power (**81, 82**).

As soon as von Rundstedt heard of the two airborne landings in the early hours of 6 June, he reckoned correctly that these defined the flanks of an intended bridgehead and he attempted to launch an immediate attack with two Panzer divisions, 12 SS and Panzer Lehr, called up on his own initiative from the general reserve. Supreme headquarters, however, promptly countermanded his order and did not release them to him until four o'clock in the afternoon; in any case, they had been held so far back that attack from the air ensured that they only arrived two days later in untidy groups. Rommel did have one division in reserve under his own command – 21 Panzer – which attacked in the afternoon of 6 June, reached the coast by the extreme eastern beachhead and even by itself could have done a good deal of damage, but for the chance of war. That evening gliders with reinforcements passed overhead and stores were parachuted to 6 Airborne Division at Pegasus bridge, and the German commander decided to withdraw in case he should be cut off, although the likelihood of this was remote.

Thus by the evening of 6 June the five beachheads had been established, although none of the major objectives had yet been gained, including Caen, which did not fall for a month. By 12 June the beachheads had been joined up and the Americans had pushed across to the west coast of the Cotentin peninsula. Once the initial lodgement had been secured, everything rested on the speed with which the two sides could build up their opposing forces. Cherbourg fell to the Allies on 26 June, but, owing to demolition carried out by the Germans, was not in use as a port for several weeks. As a consequence, the Allies had to continue to rely upon the open beaches and a floating harbour, Mulberry, which they had established at Arromanches and which had almost been put out of action in the great storm from 19 to 22 June. Even so, by 12 June the Allies had landed a third of a million men, 54,000 vehicles and 104,000 tonnes of stores; half a million men by 18 June; one million by 5 July (**10**). The Germans under constant air attack had mustered about 400,000 men, although there were many more holding the south of France, as well as the Fifteenth Army still pinned down east of the Seine by the deception plan.

Meanwhile, as the Americans pushed west and a little south, the front outside Caen in the extreme eastern sector had proved difficult to shift, mainly because the Germans were particularly anxious about its position as a road centre at the most easterly point of the bridgehead. A week after the landing there was heavy fighting to the east of Caen, when the Germans tried to dislodge the Sixth Airborne Division; also to the west of it, when the Allies failed to take Villers Bocage. Again, in the last days of June a fierce British thrust took them a little further down to the west of the city towards the river Odon and on 8 July Caen was finally captured after a devastating aerial bombardment. Ten days later Montgomery launched an offensive, code-named Goodwood, whereby an armoured attack, again preceded by an immense bombing programme from a thousand planes, thrust south of Caen towards Falaise, but it eventually came to a halt, defeated by the sheer depth of the German defences.

All this led to a bitter controversy that could well have removed Montgomery from his post – at the very moment when a group of German army officers had just failed to assassinate Hitler on 20 July (see p. 66). The failure to take Caen on the first day had meant that the British sector of the bridgehead had a depth at its east end of no more than 8 kilometres from the front to the sea. This had been resented by the air force, since it had greatly curbed their activities; it had also meant that, as the build-up of forces developed, the bridgehead had become hopelessly crowded, and the slowness of the advance had also begun to irritate the Americans, who imagined that they were being left to fight the war on their own. When the Goodwood operation petered out, indignation came to a head.

Montgomery in reply always maintained that he had not been expecting to break out in the east. This was to be done by the Americans at the extreme west end of the bridgehead, and consequently an essential feature of his strategy was to draw most of the German armour away from them over to the east (**39**). In this he could certainly claim a success, even if Operation Goodwood may not have got as far as he had hoped. On 25 July the major American assault – Operation Cobra – was launched by General Bradley at a moment when there were only two Panzer divisions and one Panzer grenadier division in front of him, while further east the British were holding seven Panzer divisions and four heavy tank battalions. By 27 July the Americans had reached Coutances; by 30 July they had broken through into Brittany at Avranches, and two American armies – Hodge's First and Patton's Third – advanced for the break-out. Within a week twelve divisions had poured through the gap, mostly driving eastwards to the south of the German Seventh Army.

Thus, the Allied front was to perform an immense left-wheeling movement, and as the British and the Canadians at the most easterly end of the front pressed down from the north, the German army seemed likely to be caught in a great pocket – named after Falaise, where the gap had to be closed. By now Hitler's officers were advising him to fall back on the Seine, but Hitler was determined to launch a counter-attack towards Mortain, striking west to the sea at Avranches to cut the Allied forces in half. All this time the Allied fighter bombers and rocket-firing Typhoons had been playing havoc with the German army in the cramped wooded countryside of this area of Normandy, the bocage, and now on 7 August, when von Kluge, who had recently replaced von Rundstedt as commander-in-chief in the west, finally opened the Mortain counter-attack, their presence was decisive. Hitler's urgent order to a hesitant von Kluge had been picked up and decoded at Bletchley and the Allies, knowing precisely where the assault was to come, stopped it in its tracks largely with air power (**16, 17**).

The German attack was renewed for several days, so that more of their forces moved into the pocket until Hitler agreed to a withdrawal on 14 August. By this time General Patton, sweeping eastwards to the south of the Germans, had been ordered to make one thrust up towards Argentan in order to meet the Canadians, who had been pushing south towards Falaise since 13 August. Air attack had already played havoc with the German forces now in retreat and the Falaise gap was finally closed on 21 August. Meanwhile, Patton's Third Army was reaching out towards the Seine and by 20 August was already over it. At the same time Allied landings in the south of France had begun on 15 August, thereby ensuring that the whole of France would soon be cleared.

The pursuit continued, but the main battle was over. Amid the litter of corpses and wreckage, the Allies could reckon that they had totally routed the German army, whose losses included some 300,000 casualties and 2,200 tanks. Almost all the armoured divisions committed to battle had been reduced to a shadow, and of von Rundstedt's original forty-eight infantry divisions, less than half were to reappear in a somewhat shattered form in September. All this had cost the Allies some 37,000 dead since 6 June (**80**).

A fortnight after the Normandy invasion, on 22 June, the Russians had launched an attack from north of the Pripet marshes on German Army Group Centre. Previous to this, Hitler had refused to withdraw from the Baltic states, a move which would have shortened his front by 480 kilometres, and consequently the German defence was soon overwhelmed. Minsk was taken on 3

July; half-way through July Marshal Koniev opened a second offensive south of the Pripet marshes and by the beginning of August reached the Vistula, while to the north Russian forces were 24 kilometres from Warsaw. This advance of 320 kilometres in the south and 480 in the centre meant that Russian communications were seriously overstretched and fierce German counter-attack brought the offensive to a halt. In all, this Russian advance, co-inciding with the campaign in France, had created a further 300,000 German casualties, and the destruction of twenty-five divisions meant the end of Army Group Centre (**74**).

Meanwhile, the western Allies were continuing their drive east-wards. By the end of August General Patton had crossed the Marne and was approaching Rheims. To the north General Horrocks, commanding thirty corps of Montgomery's 21 Army Group, was thrusting on to Amiens; by 2 September they were into Belgium; on 3 September the Guards Armoured Division entered Brussels, and on the next day Antwerp was taken so quickly by 11 Armoured Division that there was no time for the Germans to destroy the dock equipment, although they still held the estuary of the Scheldt.

Throughout these weeks a great debate had been proceeding between Montgomery and Eisenhower, who had now assumed general command of operations. Montgomery believed that it should be possible to end the war that autumn by making 'a really powerful and full-blooded thrust' over the river systems of the southern Netherlands and into Germany (**85**). Eisenhower, however, did not want to halt Patton, since he could link up with the Allied armies approaching from the landings in the south of France [**doc. 14**]. The outcome was a compromise – two prongs, whereby Montgomery was first to have his thrust across the rivers, and then Patton was to make for the Rhine.

On 17 September a massive airborne operation shot a long probing finger through Dutch territory with parachute drops and glider landings that aimed to capture the bridges over all the rivers ahead. The Americans took Eindhoven, Grave with its bridge over the Meuse, and Nijmegen with its bridge over the Waal, and the British First Airborne division dropped to the west of Arnhem aiming to capture the bridge over the lower Rhine. The bridges were intact, but everything rested now on how quickly the land forces could reach this airborne vanguard and these were hampered by the fact that they had only a single narrow road on which to operate. By 18 September they had reached Eindhoven and on 20 September they joined the Americans in the capture of Nijmegen, but by 25 September it was clear that they could not get more than half-way between Nijmegen and Arnhem. Consequently, the First Airborne were ordered to withdraw and about two thousand, one fifth of the total, managed to get away.

For the time being the Allies had lost their momentum. The American armies to the south settled down in October and November to the siege of Aachen and Metz; it took two months for the Allies to clear enemy troops from the estuary of the Scheldt, without which Antwerp was useless as a port, and all this gave the Germans time to pull together a defence force out of the ruin of their armies that had got back from Normandy. On the eastern front, too, the main Russian offensive had been checked by the beginning of August, although the Red Army had continued to feel its way forward on the southern flank and in September Bucharest and Sofia and in October Belgrade had been taken (**38**).

In December the Germans surprised all their enemies by launching a major counter-attack. The surprise was not only that they could manage such an assault with twenty divisions, seven of which were armoured, but also that it should be aimed at the west at a time when the Russians were threatening the eastern border of Germany. The attack came on 16 December, once again through the Ardennes, against the American First Army (**15**). To the north Dietrich's 6th Panzer Army was to strike for a crossing of the Meuse between Liège and Huy and to make for Antwerp, while Manteuffel's 5th Panzer Army was to make a wider sweep over the Meuse between Namur and Dinant and then on to Brussels, thereby cutting off the Allies from an important part of their base. The conception, largely Hitler's, was highly imaginative, but, as his generals saw, he lacked the resources for it. In fact, neither army reached the Meuse. Dietrich was stopped near Stavelot only half a kilometre from a vast fuel dump; Manteuffel was denied the use of two road centres at Bastogne and St Vith, which he had to bypass. By 20 December Eisenhower, realising that the Germans had now cut the American front in half, gave command of the whole of the northern sector to Montgomery – to the fury of his own generals. Montgomery reinforced the points at which he correctly guessed the Germans wished to cross the Meuse, but in his cautious way did not begin his own attack from the north until 3 January 1945, although in the south Patton had already gone into action on 22 December and had relieved Bastogne by 26 December. Only on this did Hitler decide to switch his main thrust

*The Low Countries: autumn 1944*

to Manteuffel's army, but by then it was too late and Manteuffel had run out of petrol. Finally, on 8 January 1945, Hitler agreed to give up the main assault.

The principal beneficiaries of the Ardennes counter-attack were the Russians. On 12 January Marshal Koniev's army group of 180 divisions broke through a front already weakened by the requirements in the west. The Vistula was crossed; on 17 January Warsaw was taken, and the advance only came to a halt early in February, by which time the Red Army was half-way across Hungary in the south and had reached Kuestrin on the Oder only fifty miles from Berlin (**74**).

Against the Anglo-American forces Hitler had now resolved that his main resistance must be to the west of the Rhine. To many it seemed that it would have been wiser simply to have held the east bank of the Rhine as a defence line, but Hitler knew that with the recent loss of Silesia he dared not let the Allies get too close to the Ruhr. To cope with this, Eisenhower embarked upon an equally debatable strategy – a two-pronged thrust with the British and

*The fronts of 1945*

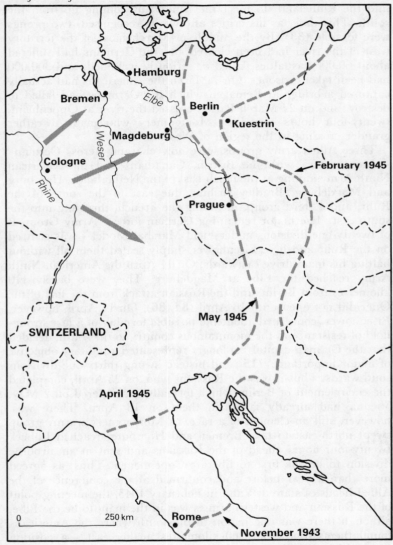

Canadians pushing down from the north through the Reichswald into the Rhineland, to meet the Americans coming up from the south. This time, as his critics afterwards recognised, two prongs were feasible (**33**). By the middle of March most of the territory west of the river had been cleared and the Germans had suffered about 60,000 casualties, killed or seriously wounded, and 300,000 had been taken prisoner. On 7 March the Americans had actually captured a bridge at Remagen which the Germans had failed to destroy, and on 22 March Patton crossed the river at Oppenheim, twenty-four hours ahead of Montgomery who made a rather grander crossing in the region of Wesel.

Three Allied army groups were now charging across Germany – Montgomery with the British, Canadians and the American Ninth Army aiming at the north-east of the Netherlands, Hamburg and Magdeburg; Bradley rushing due east to the south of the Ruhr; and a third group, including the French, thrusting into the south-east. The major remaining German force – Army Group B of twenty-one divisions under Field Marshal Model – was centred on the Ruhr and here Eisenhower simply sealed them off without halting his main drive eastwards. On 11 April the American Ninth Army reached the Elbe at Magdeburg. They were barely 110 kilometres from Berlin, and the Russian attack from the line of the Oder did not open until 16 April (**84, 86**). On 14 April, however, Eisenhower, concerned about the possible forming of a last stronghold of resistance in the mountainous country to the south, decided that the German capital 'no longer represented a military objective of major importance' (**15**) and instead swung thirty-one divisions southwards. Thus it was the Russians who, on 25 April, completed the encirclement of Berlin, which formally surrendered on 2 May. Vienna had already fallen to them on 13 April. There was, however, still an element of a race, as Montgomery's army group swept north-east to take Bremen and Hamburg, reached Lübeck twenty-four hours ahead of the Russians and sent in an airborne division to be the first to liberate Copenhagen. Thus, as agreed more than a year before and confirmed at the conference of the Allied heads of state at Yalta in February 1945, the meeting point of the Russian and western armies was in the main to be the Elbe, although there was one region to the south where the Americans found themselves about 160 kilometres further east – a position from which they withdrew that summer.

On 30 April Hitler committed suicide in his bunker in the grounds of the chancellery in Berlin, having nominated Admiral

Doenitz as his successor. A local surrender had already taken place in Italy; another followed on Lüneberg Heath, when Montgomery received that of all German forces in north-west Europe; and on 7 May, at Eisenhower's headquarters at Rheims, General Jodl and Admiral von Friedeburg signed a document of total unconditional surrender before representatives of the United States, Great Britain, France and Russia [**doc. 15**].

# Part Three:  Strategic Factors

## 7  The Command of the Air

With the development of aircraft, warfare in the twentieth century acquired a third dimension. The First World War had merely given a glimpse of this potential; the Second enshrined it as a vital element in the strategic and tactical pattern. The existence of Fighter Command was the key to survival for Great Britain in the summer of 1940, and throughout the war the RAF's Coastal Command formed part of the general defence of her home waters. Indeed, it soon became clear that all kinds of shipping were extremely vulnerable to attack from the air and the British themselves relied largely upon this, when the supply convoys for the Afrikakorps were harassed from Malta. For the military the immediate purpose was tactical, since an air force could provide a protective umbrella for their operations, as it did in Africa, Italy and Normandy and on the eastern front, although the Allies never developed as close a co-ordination as was needed for the German concept of *Blitzkrieg* (**23**).

As has been seen (p. 4) the prevailing doctrine among senior airmen in Great Britain during the inter-war years had demanded an overwhelming bomber offensive, which would be sufficient to achieve victory on its own. Churchill himself never believed that this could be the sole method for defeating the enemy. 'I deprecate placing unbounded confidence in this means of attack,' he wrote to the chief of the air staff, Air Chief Marshal Sir Charles Portal, in October 1941, '. . . if the United States enters the war, it would have to be supplemented in 1943 by simultaneous attacks by armoured forces in many of the conquered countries which were ripe for revolt. Even if all the towns of Germany were rendered uninhabitable, it does not follow that the military control would be weakened, or even that war industry could not be carried on.' In the event, however, the enthusiasts had their way, since after the summer of 1940 aerial bombardment represented the only means whereby Great Britain could strike directly and immediately at Germany.

This was the origin of the immense strategic air offensive which

Great Britain, later joined by the Americans, unleashed with increasing strength over the years. In Germany city after city was reduced to mountains of rubble. Over six million homes were destroyed or severely damaged, and some 600,000 civilians were killed. For the attackers, too, the cost was appalling; in the British Bomber Command alone nearly 56,000 air crew were lost – a figure which may be compared with the 70,000 German air crew killed on all fronts throughout the war (**6**).

The full weight of this assault only developed in the last years, Until the end of 1941 the British offensive had not been particularly effective. Their bombs were not big enough; they suffered serious losses with their initial attempts at selective attacks on targets in daylight, and when after April 1940 they switched to night attack, their bombing became extremely inaccurate, while German anti-aircraft fire and night fighters still inflicted considerable losses. From February 1942, however, under Air Marshal Harris there was a deliberate change of policy to concentrating on area bombing in the hope that the general destruction of cities would affect the morale of the German people. Throughout 1942 and 1943, with the aid of new designs – the Lancaster, the Halifax, the Mosquito and the American Flying Fortress – new navigational aids and new techniques, such as the use of the Pathfinder force of expert crews who went ahead to mark the target with flares, the cities of Germany came under a growing volume of ever larger bombs – the Ruhr from March to July 1943, Hamburg from July to November 1943, and Berlin from November 1943 to March 1944.

All this represented the use of air power as an independent weapon in its own right and there was considerable argument in high places before agreement could be reached over temporarily diverting this effort to the destruction of the railway system in north-eastern France as a preliminary to the Normandy invasion. It has been seen (p. 32) that the devastation caused by this and the continuing control of the air over the battlefield were vital factors in the Allies' victory there. In the summer of 1944, however, the strategic air force shifted back to what was regarded as its principal objectives and with air fields now available in France an overwhelming weight of bombs continued to fall on industrial cities, oil fields and synthetic oil plants, until the armies of Russia and the west had met in the middle of Germany.

The whole strategic air offensive was riddled with controversy. One issue was the choice of area bombing, as opposed to a concentration on individual targets. Long after the war, the moral aspect of this predominated, but at the time, in the atmosphere of a struggle for survival, it did not have great impact. The German bombing of Warsaw on 24 and 25 September 1939, Rotterdam on 14 May 1940, and London and many cities in the English provinces in the autumn of 1940 appeared to make it an acceptable means of war, although the destruction of Dresden in February 1945 did raise some objections even at the time.

A more practical feature of the controversy was whether a concentration of attack on particular targets, such as the Möhne dam in May 1943, U-boat bases and German factories producing aircraft, would not have been more telling. The immediate answer would be that the Allies had turned to area bombing precisely because, in 1940 and 1941, they had not succeeded in hitting selected targets with sufficient accuracy, and in any case these had often proved too well defended. The Möhne dam raid, for instance, had cost eight out of nineteen Lancasters. Nevertheless, there is no escape from the fact that the area bombing campaign did not achieve its immediate object either. German civilian morale did not crack and by dispersing factories over the countryside throughout 1943 and with the use of slave labour that could be worked to death, Albert Speer, Hitler's minister of war production, achieved a remarkable increase in the production of all war materials, which reached a peak as late as July 1944, after which the mounting Allied assault did take its toll (see p. 55).

Quite apart from the question of area or precision bombing, the strategic air offensive has come under criticism from another angle. It has been suggested that its goal was wrongly conceived, since its planners had ignored a cardinal principle of war that the first objective must be the destruction of the corresponding enemy force. Consequently, Allied air power should have been aimed directly at the Luftwaffe itself. As it was, the Allies did not achieve supremacy in the air until spring 1944. This delay, however, may not have been the direct result of concentrating on bombing, but rather a slowness is coming to grips with the problem of providing bombers with fighters to protect them. Even when this was done, the fighters were at first inadequate to deal with the German night fighters and it was not until December 1943 that the Mustang, with its greater range, speed and manoeuvrability, first went into action with the American Eighth Air Force, although it could have been in production long before.

And lastly, apart from its methods and aims, the very conception of an independent strategic air offensive in itself has been the subject of doubts which Churchill had expressed earlier. All arms of the services were vital for the attainment of victory. They were also vital to each other and no single one could win the war alone, whatever its members might think. In theory the destruction of the enemy's means of making war might seem the most economical strategy, yet the onslaught on German oil supply did not come close to fulfilling the original plan until September 1944, when oil output was reduced to a quarter. By this time, however, other requirements had been met. The Allied air force had gained a positive supremacy over its opponent. And the bombers in this last phase could all be based in France, as a result of the victory in Normandy, in which the air force, temporarily abandoning its independent role, had played an essential part. Thus the fortunes of the air force and the army appeared to be inextricably inter-woven, and the more ambitious aims of the air offensive could only be achieved when the claims of some of its critics had been satisfied.

# 8   The Command of the Sea

The command of the sea was economic and strategic in its significance − economic, as each side attempted to shut off all imports
from the enemy; strategic, in that the launching and sustaining of
overseas operations depended utterly upon it. Unlike the question
of the air offensive, however, all this was seen from the start as a
form of combined operation, since aircraft were a vital element to
be used alongside surface and submarine sea forces (**5**).

At particular moments in the war specific areas of the sea were
bound to have an importance of their own. Clearly in 1940 and
1944 sea power in the Channel was crucial, although in May 1940
the assessment of the chiefs of staff reckoned that the British navy
could only hold off invasion for a limited time, if there were not
also corresponding control of the air [**doc. 2**]. In the spring of 1943
the Allied naval supremacy in the Mediterranean meant that the
Axis forces bottled up in Tunisia were doomed. From September
1941 the Arctic convoys to Murmansk suffered appalling losses,
but 720 ships in all managed to get through out of a total of 811,
and there was political as well as practical significance in the four
million tonnes of supplies, including 5,000 tanks and 7,000 aircraft,
that they brought to Russia.

The most significant area throughout the war was the Atlantic.
Across this most of Great Britain's imports of food, munitions and
petroleum had to come; and until the Mediterranean was opened
up, nearly all reinforcements and supply for the British Army in
Egypt had to pass down the west coast of Africa and round the
Cape. A neutral Eire would not allow the use of any of her Atlantic
ports, and, once France had fallen, the vast bulk of shipping had
to enter the United Kingdom through the narrows of the north-
western approaches between Scotland and Northern Ireland,
where the wolf packs of German U-boats lay in wait for them.

As well as using mines, the Germans made some use of surface
craft to destroy enemy ships. In the autumn of 1939 their pocket
battleship *Graf Spee* had a short season in the Atlantic, sinking
merchantmen, before she was chased into Montevideo, where she

was scuttled. The cruiser *Admiral Hipper* also made a couple of successful trips. In 1941 the battle cruisers *Scharnhorst* and *Gneisenau* achieved a number of sinkings, but the greatest excitement of that year was when the battleship *Bismarck* got loose in the Atlantic, which she could have dominated, thereby stimulating a great concentration of British forces which were able to sink her on 26 May.

In the main, however, the Germans relied upon U-boats under the control of Admiral Doenitz, who eventually, in January 1943, took over the supreme command of the navy from Admiral Raeder. The principal problem for the Germans here was that they had started the war with a very small submarine force (see p. 2) and it was not until the end of 1941 that Hitler was prepared to consider any great increase. This was precisely the period when the British were at their weakest. They had put a garrison into Iceland, which was a helpful stepping-stone, but it was only in the summer of 1941 that they were able to afford escort vessels to accompany convoys of merchantmen the whole way across the Atlantic, and until April 1943 there were still 480 kilometres in the middle of the journey where no air cover was possible. Thus, during these early years the British could have lost the battle of the Atlantic, but the German admirals did not have the U-boat strength that they needed to accomplish this (**28**).

Nevertheless, they made their impact. In 1939, over 200 merchant ships were sunk, a tonnage of 755,000, more than half by U-boat; in 1940, 1,000 ships of nearly four million tonnage; in 1941, 1,200 ships of over four million tonnage. To achieve these formidable figures the Germans tracked a convoy until it was beyond air cover and then attacked at night on the surface, where Asdic (see p. 3) was useless against them. Even so, they were a very long way off the 700,000 tonnage a month that Raeder and Doenitz reckoned that they needed if their blockade was to succeed, and throughout this time the number of operational U-boats grew only very slowly – forty-six in April 1940, sixty-five in July 1941, ninety-one in January 1942.

The Battle of the Atlantic was significant in another way in that it was the theatre in which Anglo-American co-operation was most noticeable. Although, theoretically, the United States was neutral until December 1941, the American government had handed over in September 1940 fifty old destroyers in return for eight British bases in the West Indies, and in March 1941 the provisions of the Lend-Lease Act enabled Great Britain to draw enormously on

American production. In the Atlantic itself there was an even more practical commitment, as the Americans provided more and more of the escorting on the western side of the ocean, established air bases in Greenland and took over the garrisoning of Reykjavik in Iceland (see p. 76).

This American involvement was bound to be much greater after Hitler's declaration of war in December 1941 (see p. 22), yet it was only then that the German government began to reinforce its effort in the Atlantic. Throughout 1942 over 1,600 ships – a tonnage of nearly seven million – were sunk, mostly caught in that gap where no air cover was available. This was faster than the Allies could build them and by the end of the year Doenitz had over 200 U-boats operational. It was in these hazardous circumstances that the landings in North Africa were launched and it was hardly surprising that the Allies in conference at Casablanca in January 1943 decided that until the German threat in the Atlantic had been ended, no major invasion of the Continent would be possible. This view seemed to be confirmed, when in February the German sinkings surpassed 600,000 tonnes and in March almost reached 700,000, the figure that the German admirals had established as their target.

If all this had happened two years earlier, it might have had a decisive effect upon the course of the war. As it was, it came too late for the Germans. March 1943 was to be their peak. In April very long-range Liberators operating from Iceland and Newfoundland were able to close the gap in the air cover in mid-ocean. Until now, Allied aircraft had relied upon a long-wave radar to discover U-boats on the surface, but this could be detected by the Germans, who then had time to dive out of sight. They were, however, unable to detect a new very short-wave radar – H2S – which was now introduced, and this proved to be deadly. At the same time special naval groups had been formed actively to hunt the U-boats, using the convoys as bait and following the direction of a scouting aircraft equipped with the new radar (**11, 18**).

The consequence of this great concentration by the Allies in the Atlantic came with dramatic suddenness. In April 1943 the figures for sinkings by the Germans dropped by 300,000 tonnes. In May Doenitz was reporting a serious crisis to Hitler and between June and August only fifty-eight Allied ships were sunk, whereas seventy-nine U-boats were lost. And so the trend was to continue until, by the time the Allies launched the Normandy invasion, the command of the sea was securely in their hands.

# 9 Intelligence and Secret Weapons

An intelligence service seeks to provide each commander in the field with a knowledge of the disposition, strength and suspected intentions of the forces opposing him, and for this there has to be a constant observation of the enemy's order of battle, i.e. the changing layout of his forces over the whole theatre of the war, together with the nature of the units which they comprise, the names and background of the enemy commanders and the details of supply and distribution. It also attempts to keep pace with or to anticipate the development of new weapons or technological devices, so that they can be countered as soon as they are used.

In the front line the normal means of gaining local information was through reconnaissance patrols. Prisoners might unwittingly reveal odd fragments of the jigsaw when interrogated, and unguarded conversations amongst themselves could be picked up in a variety of ways. On a wider scale aerial photography became increasingly precise during the war and many resistance groups in the occupied countries were eventually provided with secret radio links with London or personal links through agents landed by air or sea. All these means were important in locating radar stations and the construction sites and experimental areas for the V1 flying bombs and V2 rockets on the Baltic coast and in Poland. It was Russian partisans who unmasked a German deception plan before the Battle of Kursk in July 1943, and there was a regular flow of information from northern France and Belgium on German dispositions before the Normandy invasion.

One refinement of intelligence was to take over the enemy's communications system and to use it against him. A successful instance of this happened in 1942, when a wireless set and its London codes used by the Dutch resistance were captured by the Germans. For over a year they then organised the dispatch of fifty-two British agents to the Netherlands, and arrested all of them immediately they arrived (**7**). The British too were successful in rounding up most German spies in Great Britain, many of whom were then set to work sending back false information. This was immensely helpful in organising the deception plan for Normandy in 1944 (see p. 31) and in confusing the Germans over the accuracy of their V2 rockets later that year (**18**).

Naturally, the real key to intelligence was the breaking of the enemy codes and both sides had some success in this respect. The Germans were reading the ciphers of the British Navy in the early part of the war and the Italians at one stage broke an American cipher. There is, however, no parallel to the story of the Enigma machine and the use which the Ultra organisation at Bletchley made of it (see p. 3). The record here is extraordinary. German tactics in the Battle of Britain, Rommel's dispositions in the desert, the sailing of his supply convoys across the Mediterranean, his plan of attack at Alam Halfa, the Mortain counter-attack in Normandy, all these were revealed in time for the Allies to devise their own plans in the light of the information (**16, 17**).

Indeed, the assistance given by Ultra was so remarkable that it is reasonable to wonder why the Allies suffered so long from defeat during the early years of the war. Ultra, however, could not be infallible. The Germans frequently changed the operating wheels of their machine and there were periods when the decoders could not translate the messages in time, even with the aid of elaborate, although relatively primitive, computers. In any case, intelligence alone cannot win a war and at first much of what was picked up may simply have confirmed the weak position of the Allies. Or, if the Germans practised a radio silence and relied mainly on telephone communication by line, as happened before the Ardennes counter-attack in December 1944, then Ultra could know very little. Or sometimes, as over the Battle of Crete, the information does not seem to have been acted upon. Apart from this, however, there was one other inhibiting factor in the use made of the information. If it had become too apparent that the Allies were reading the German signals, then the Germans would have abandoned Enigma, leaving their enemies totally in the dark, and this would have been a serious setback for the fortunes of the eventual cross-Channel invasion, the operation that had to succeed if the war was to be won. Consequently, when information from Enigma was acted upon, there often had to be an elaborate pretence that it had been discovered in some other way. In fact, the Germans could never quite bring themselves to believe that their coding had been broken and when their enemy did seem to know too much, they put it down to carelessness on the part of the Italians.

As well as a race for information, there was also a race to invent new weapons to which the enemy had no counter. Much of this effort went into modifications and improvements in the design of mines, tanks, aeroplanes or guns, such as the German 88 mm gun or the German Tiger and Panther tanks, or, on the Allied side, the long-range Liberator, the Mustang and the rocket-firing Typhoon. Equally, the prospect of invasion stimulated the Allies to design a wide variety of landing craft and the floating harbour Mulberry.

The exploration of more esoteric methods led to what Winston Churchill called the 'Wizard War'. In the course of the Battle of Britain Dr R. V. Jones's scientific intelligence unit had established that German bombers were being guided to their targets by radio beams, which he was then able to distort. In 1942 the British designed their own aid to aircraft navigation, a system known as Gee, and later one still more sophisticated, known as Oboe. By the end of the second year of the war the Germans had created a chain of radar stations from Denmark to the south-west corner of France and the position of these was carefully plotted by the British over the years, so that they could be dealt with before the invasion, some to be destroyed, some to be jammed and some to be left to collect the false clues of the deception plan (see p. 31). By 1942 both sides had thought of a means of confusing their opponent's radar by dropping reflecting material, known by the Allies as 'Window', but both held back for a year from using it for fear of giving the idea to the other side – a good example of some of the psychological complexities created by this aspect of the war. For the British the most striking development was a radar bombing aid, known as H2S, which enabled the navigator to discern the contour of town and country at night. And as has been seen, this was also invaluable in the last stages of the Battle of the Atlantic (see p. 48) (**18**).

Naturally, all new devices had only a limited life before the enemy discovered how to neutralise them. Jones had reckoned that Gee would be jammed within three months, although it actually survived for five. In the same way the Germans would probably have found a means of protecting their U-boats against H2S, but the Battle of the Atlantic had been lost before they could do so, and after that the German retreat from France deprived them of their western naval bases.

Two major instruments of war were never actually put into operation in Europe. Gas, the great dread of the inter-war years, was thought to be too unreliable, or would have caused too much devastation on each side. The Allies also undertook research into

51

the making of an atom bomb, not originally intending to use it, but merely in order to have a counter, in case the Germans succeeded in making one. As it was, the Germans made little progress in this direction and the atom bomb was never exploded in the European theatre. Hitler talked constantly of secret weapons, but he seems to have been thinking principally of the V1 flying bomb and the V2 rocket, which in the summer and autumn of 1944 did create considerable havoc in English cities. Scientific intelligence, however, had picked up fragments of evidence about these during the period of experiment and the Allied air attacks on the sites put back their launching at least until after the Normandy invasion had begun – another aspect of the significance of time in these operations.

# 10    The Economics of War

Behind the struggle on land, sea and air lay the imponderables of economic power, and in this field each of the combatants was to develop their potential in a different way. At the time it was assumed in the west that by 1939 Hitler's Germany had been placed totally on a war footing; in fact, as was discovered afterwards, there had been no general reorganising of the German economy for war at all. Certainly Hitler had rearmed; in 1938 nearly 25 per cent of his national income had been spent on armaments – in contrast to Great Britain's 7 per cent – but this had been achieved simply through placing orders with the armaments industry, as with any other commodity. He had no wish to establish a plan for a comprehensive war economy. That would have implied a lengthy period of hostilities, which he was convinced would be beyond Germany's strength. Instead, he envisaged the sharp shock of *Blitzkrieg*. Not merely would the shortness of this make it unnecessary to place the economy on a war footing, but there would be a positive advantage, since the defeating of each successive opponent might demand different forms of weapons, and it was reckoned that the requisite flexibility would be best provided by the existing structure of German industry acting on the commands of the Führer, who would also allocate the necessary raw materials (**24**).

Thus for the first two years of the war Germany adopted a policy of armament 'in breadth' which did not require any control over civilian manpower and left the output of consumer goods largely unaffected. Naturally this policy had some critics. General Georg Thomas deplored the lack of central planning, and Albert Speer, later Minister of Armaments and Munitions, maintained afterwards that the absence of a long-term economic plan from the beginning of the war was the reason for Germany's eventual collapse. Yet the record of those early years made it difficult for any criticism to carry conviction. German successes in Poland, Norway and France, and even in the early stages of the Russian campaign in 1941, as they thrust towards the Ukraine and Moscow, all suggested that armament 'in breadth' was not only adequate, but perhaps the most appropriate means. At the same time the victories now put the raw materials and production of most of the Continent at Germany's disposal (**31**).

When the 1941 onslaught petered out, however, it seemed that *Blitzkrieg* had run its course, and Hitler was confronted with a prolonged war eventually to be fought on two fronts, the very situation that he had always hoped to avoid. The prospect of a war of attrition meant the end of armament 'in breadth', and now a belated armament 'in depth' was to open up the new phase in Germany's economic effort. The first to attempt this was Fritz Todt, who had become Minister for Armaments and Munitions in March 1940, but he had been able to make very little headway against the climate of opinion until December 1941 when Hitler began to issue a series of Führer commands which were at last to bring about a total mobilisation for war. In February 1942 Todt was killed in an air crash and was replaced at once by Albert Speer, who held the position until the end of the war (**51**). In April a central planning board was established, but much of Speer's energy was taken up in battling with German army agencies and with the other services; the navy did not allow him to deal with their production until the middle of 1943; the air force not until March 1944. The supply of labour, including the importing of millions of slave workers from the occupied countries, remained in the hands of another department throughout the war – a fact which may have helped to save Speer's life at the Nuremberg tribunal afterwards.

Nevertheless, the dynamic supplied by Hitler and Speer did bring about a revolution in military supply, much to the surprise of the Allies who had imagined that Germany had already reached her peak in the first years of the war. Between February 1942 and July 1944 the production of armaments and aircraft increased by three times, and within that growth that of tanks went up six times and hand armaments nearly four times. Yet, despite Speer's efforts, there were few cuts in civilian consumption throughout this period. Still more remarkable, the increased output was all achieved against the crescendo of the Allied air offensive through extensive programmes of dispersal, coupled with a strengthening of the defences of the factories that could not be shifted. A number of errors, however, did detract from the full effect of the expansion. Hitler was determined to concentrate on quality, but was inclined to spread this over too many different models, with the result that there was always a shortage of spare parts. Determined to hit back, he still favoured the construction of bombers long after the time when it would have been wiser to have built up the number of defensive fighters; and the V1 and V2 missiles, to which he pinned his faith, used up electrical equipment badly needed by U-boats and radar.

Only after the Normandy invasion would Hitler allow Speer at last to concentrate on the mass production of a few standard models and it is the measure of Speer's ability that as late as September 1944 he managed to turn out 3,538 planes (in contrast to 2,316 in June 1943). But by now time was running out. Allied bombing of German oil plants meant that there was insufficient fuel to fly these planes. The production of coal and steel and the use of roads and railways were also seriously affected. The occupied territories, which had supplied men and materials, had now been regained by the Allies and in his last months of power Speer was more interested in frustrating Hitler's orders for a policy of scorched earth.

In contrast to Germany, the British and French governments reckoned from the start that they were faced with the prospect of a long war and that they must consequently take some time in building up an economic mobilisation in depth, while Germany could be held at bay by means of the Maginot line and a naval blockade. Both countries made thorough arrangements about food, shipping and armaments, but there was not a great deal of co-operation between them and the pace generally was leisurely.

It was the fall of France that galvanised the British effort – a stimulus of which Albert Speer later spoke with some envy. All their resources had now to be exploited to the full, as they settled down to a state of siege under Churchill, but apart from the concentration on the production of fighter aircraft during the emergency of the Battle of Britain, the emphasis was still on long-term planning. The chief supervisory body for this was the Lord President's Committee under a civil servant, Sir John Anderson, and although there was considerable reliance upon voluntary co-operation, the government rapidly acquired a far more totalitarian grip than either of its totalitarian opponents. This covered the whole range of materials and labour as well as military service, and by the middle of 1944 one third of the total labour force was employed in war work – including over two million women. Between 1940 and 1942 Great Britain produced more tanks and aircraft than Germany, and the weight of taxation was such that even by 1944, 55 per cent of government expenditure was being financed out of current revenue – in comparison with Germany's 23 per cent. The amount of land under cultivation rose from under 5 million to over 7 million hectares (**10**).

Nevertheless, it is extremely unlikely that Great Britain alone could have coped with the economic power of Germany who soon had nearly all the continent of Europe on which to draw. In this context the American contribution was bound to be crucial, but its availability was to depend upon a number of factors. By August 1940 President Roosevelt had come to see that the continuing resistance to Germany by Great Britain was well worth American support, and in March 1941 the British shortage of dollars was overcome by an Act of Congress authorising the system of Lend-Lease (**21**). This allowed the President to supply war material to any country thought to be playing a significant part in the defence of the United States, while any payment could be postponed at the President's discretion. In 1941 this gave Great Britain 750 million dollars' worth of material. American public opinion, however, was nervous about the apparent likelihood of being drawn into the war, and Roosevelt had to act more cautiously over the protecting of the Atlantic convoys that delivered these goods (see p. 76).

Naturally Hitler's declaration of war in December 1941 removed all need of hesitation and from then on the American economic involvement was prodigious. Between 1939 and 1945 the total production of all materials doubled, while within this broad increase transportation equipment went up seven times and machinery four times. The loss of the rubber-producing regions to the Japanese resulted in the establishment of over fifty factories for synthetic rubber, which by the middle of 1944 were producing 50 per cent more than the amount of natural rubber imported before the war. In merchant ship building a tonnage of three million was launched in 1942 and of nine million in 1943. For the supply of the services 86,000 tanks were built during the war and 64,500 landing craft; naval vessels rose from 4,500 to 91,000, and aircraft from 8,000 to 120,000. Of personnel, service recruitment brought the total number by May 1945 to twelve million, of whom over eight million were in the army.

The finance for all this had to be voted by Congress, who as early as 1941 had authorised an expenditure of fifty thousand million dollars for the year. By June 1943 this had risen to nearly 8,000 million a month; in all, 186 thousand million dollars were spent on munitions, and a total of forty-three thousand million on Lend-Lease, two thirds of which went to Great Britain and a quarter to Russia. The statistics are endless, but these few may give some idea of the economic potential that Hitler with one decision had turned against himself.

Thus far, it is clear that Great Britain and the United States only embarked upon a full-blooded exploitation of their economy after they had been drawn into war, and even after the outbreak Germany avoided a total economic mobilisation until the end of 1941. For the Soviet Union the pattern was very different. This was only natural, since under a Communist regime a massive state planning of the economy was as normal a feature of peace-time as it would be of war-time. At first Russia's relations with Germany had remained ostensibly good and the pact of August 1939 over the partition of Poland had been followed in February 1940 by a trade treaty that enabled Germany to buy immense supplies of grain, oil and timber from her.

Historically, Russia had always had to reckon on the threat of invasion from the west, and an essential element in her defence had been the sheer extent of her territory which could soak up any invading force across the steppes of European Russia. This temporary loss of territory, however, could easily deprive her of the industrial means for continuing the war, and consequently another economic base had to be established beyond the reach of the invader. Hence the eventual survival of Russia in the Second World War was to depend upon the measures taken with this in mind before the German attack began. Between 1938 and 1941 under the third Five-Year Plan an immense industrial development of mines and factories was organised to the east of the Urals and by June 1941 39 per cent of Russia's steel, 35 per cent of her coal, 25 per cent of her electricity and 50 per cent of her tractors came from Siberia (**74**).

Even so, the process was by no means complete when Hitler struck and as his forces pushed east, hundreds of factories in his path were hurriedly dismantled and reassembled on the far side of the Urals. Such a dislocation was bound to mean an immediate drop in output, but this was short-lived, and by 1942 Russia was turning out 2,000 tanks and 3,000 aircraft a month. None of this could have been achieved without the most rigorous mobilisation of available labour power, now greatly reduced by the millions needed for the army and by more millions cut off behind the German lines. Women were conscripted as well as men and by 1943 they formed 53 per cent of the work-force, and on the farms 71 per cent. Agriculture was in some ways the most difficult aspect of Russian supply; new lands were opened up in the east, but they lacked the fertility of the Black Earth regions of the Ukraine, which had not been cleared of the enemy before the end of 1943. The industrial base east of the Urals, however, remained secure and was one vital factor in the eventual Russian recovery.

# 11 Logistics: Cross-Channel Invasion versus the Mediterranean Campaign

From the moment when Hitler invaded Russia the Soviet government never ceased to demand that the west should open a second front across the Channel as a diversion that might assist them. Once the Anglo-American alliance had been formed, it was agreed that the defeat of Germany should have priority over that of Japan [**doc. 7b**] and that the service chiefs of both countries should form a team, the combined chiefs of staff, to plan for this. Even with the strategic and economic forces at their disposal, however, a return to the Continent would be so formidable an operation that there was considerable divergence of view how it was to be done. The argument that ensued is of considerable significance for later generations, since it centred round the projected date for a cross-Channel invasion. If this had been successfully effected in 1943, it should have meant an earlier end to the war; many Jews and Slavs would have been saved from extermination, and with Smolensk, Orel, Kharkov and Taganrog in German hands in July 1943, the Red Army would still have been fighting on Russian soil. Thus the subsequent meeting point with the Anglo-American forces might well have been as far east as the Vistula, and the post-war scene in eastern Europe would have been radically different from what emerged after the Normandy invasion of 1944. It is therefore important to ask what considerations prevented a cross-Channel invasion in 1943 and to assess what chances of success it might have had, if it had been launched then.

The eventual exclusion of the 1943 possibility emanated unwittingly from a comprehensive plan for the future sketched by Churchill on his way across the Atlantic to meet Roosevelt at the Washington conference in December 1941. The principal feature of this was that the immediate objective for the Allies in 1942 should be landings in French North-West Africa, where some of the Allied forces could come direct from the United States. This would open up the Mediterranean, relieve the Allies of the long haul round the Cape and foster Axis uncertainty about their southern regions. At the same time, air power was to be increased by the stationing of American bomber squadrons in Great Britain. All this would be a preliminary to a variety of landings on the Continent in 1943, when it was hoped that the populations under occupation would be encouraged to rise in revolt [**doc. 7a**].

The American chiefs of staff headed by General Marshall did not care for this plan. They believed that after their experience of the Battle of France in 1940 the British were nervous of a direct confrontation with the Germans in a cross-Channel invasion and were using the North African scheme as a means of postponing it. Consequently, in March 1942, Marshall put to Roosevelt an alternative proposal that all preparations must be aimed at a cross-Channel invasion in April 1943. In his view a North African adventure would merely mean a dangerous dispersal of effort, whereas the British Isles offered a perfect base for a great concentration of power and the only point from where the Allies could utilise their strength in the air [**doc. 7c**].

Before long, the British chiefs of staff were sympathetic to this, although they and the war cabinet were opposed to a further American suggestion that there should be a quick assault across the Channel in 1942, if either Germany or Russia showed signs of weakening. Later the Americans themselves blew cold on the idea of a preliminary invasion, since this might interfere with the plans for the main one in 1943; but so, too, they argued, would the proposed North African landing, and there came a point when the chiefs of staff of each country seemed agreed that both operations should be abandoned for the sake of an invasion of France in 1943.

Roosevelt and Churchill, however, were determined that there should be action somewhere in 1942, if only for political reasons. To them it was vital that there should at least be a gesture of support towards Russia. Furthermore, if nothing were planned for 1942, the Pacific lobby in the United States might well gain a large transfer of forces to the war against the Japanese. Thus, in July 1942 the American joint chiefs of staff arrived in London with orders from their President to carry out some course of action in 1942 – either a cross-Channel invasion or the North African landings. The British were adamant that there could be no invasion in 1942; the fact that Rommel had just pushed the Eighth Army as far back as El Alamein strengthened their argument, and accordingly agreement was reached to go ahead with the North African landings instead – Operation Torch – with the proviso that this was only to take place if Russia seemed likely to collapse by 15 September.

The inclusion of this condition marked a last desperate effort by the American joint chiefs of staff to avoid what they regarded as an incorrect policy, although pressure from their President had left them with little option but to silence their original objections to Torch. They did also give expression to their irritation by declaring that Torch had probably made a cross-Channel invasion impossible even in 1943. The British chiefs of staff were less wholehearted in their support of this last view and Churchill positively disagreed with it. Anyway, Roosevelt had now got the promise of action that he wanted and on 30 July 1942, ignoring the proviso about the imminence of Russian collapse, he gave a positive order for Torch to take place, in his capacity as American commander-in-chief. Thus Churchill's plan for the landings in French North Africa took effect because the British chiefs of staff would not agree to a cross-Channel invasion in 1942 and the American President was prepared to overrule his own chiefs of staff (**1**).

Nevertheless, the arguments which they put forward remain valid. Largely as a consequence of the commitments entered into in 1942 there was no cross-Channel invasion in 1943. Operations along the north coast of Africa did drag on, since Montgomery's advance westwards after the battle of El Alamein was so slow and cautious that Rommel was able to carry out a fighting retreat. Over the landings in Algeria the Americans, in contrast to their optimism about an operation across the Channel, were anxious not to strike too far along the coast, at Bône for instance, and thus the German army was able to fall back on Tunisia for a last stand, where resistance continued until 13 May 1943.

The commitment in North Africa, however, was not the sole reason for ruling out any hope of a cross-Channel invasion in 1943. It was also the consequence of the formulation of new plans with different priorities. In January 1943, at the Anglo-American conference at Casablanca, General Sir Alan Brooke, the chairman of the British chiefs of staff committee, outlined a proposal for positively continuing the Mediterranean strategy, using North Africa as a base for attacking Sardinia or Italy or the Balkan coast [**doc. 11**]. The strategic potential of the Mediterranean area had already been stressed by Churchill at a meeting at Chequers a week after the North African landings had begun, when he spoke of striking at the underbelly of the Axis. Later there was a tendency to talk about 'the soft underbelly', although the Mediterranean regions of the European continent were anything but soft, as the troops in Italy were to discover, and this later precluded any deep involvement in the Balkans.

Brooke was convinced that Mediterranean operations were an essential preliminary to any invasion elsewhere. Attack here, it was argued, would certainly be the quickest way of providing relief for Russia, and it might bring Turkey into the war on the side of the Allies. It might, too, knock Italy out of the war, although there was some doubt over how this would come about. Eden reckoned that it would be difficult for her government to make any formal surrender, since the Germans could almost certainly carry out an occupation as soon as they suspected such a move. Churchill, on the other hand, was characteristically optimistic over the chances of bringing about the fall of Mussolini. So far as Brooke was concerned, a German occupation was to be desired, since it would present the Germans with the greater logistic problems of moving north-south, and as the Allied threat developed, more German divisions would be drawn into Italy and thus would not be available in north-west Europe, when the cross-Channel invasion was eventually launched.

All this interest in continuing the Mediterranean strategy, coupled with some hard facts about comparative German and Allied strength, eventually pushed the American chiefs of staff into agreement. Major planning concentrated on the attack on Sicily, and a cross-Channel invasion for 1943 became increasingly improbable, although in the planners' memorandum there was some token reference to the possibility of establishing a bridge-head in north-west Europe, if the opportunity presented itself. Thus Brooke had gained his principal objective, although one consequence was that the American Pacific lobby was now able to gain the transfer of some shipping and troops for operations in Burma [**doc. 11**].

In this way the general pattern of the war, with the likelihood of no invasion until 1944, was established at Casablanca. This has been deplored by one critic, John Grigg, who maintains that if the campaigning had been speedier along the North African coast and if the German forces in Tunisia had merely been contained and starved out, it should have been possible to switch all Allied efforts to a cross-Channel invasion in 1943 and thus gain the advantages of an earlier end to the war (**19**).

Of course, all this assumes that such an invasion in 1943 would have been successful and on this, too, there is considerable disagreement. Grigg's belief in the success of the operation is based on the extent of air power and manpower at the disposal of the Allies; he argues that there were sufficient landing craft available, since there were more involved in the attack on Sicily in July 1943 than were eventually used in Normandy in June 1944; the Atlantic wall was less well defended in 1943; the technical devices, such as the floating Mulberry harbour, could have been developed in time for a 1943 operation; and since the German army in the east would still have been fighting on Russian soil, German east-west communications would have been much longer to meet a new threat in the west.

On the whole, this hypothesis has not met with acceptance. Chester Wilmot, very critical of other aspects of Allied policy (see p. 66), does not seriously contemplate the possibility of a 1943 invasion and others have reckoned that such an attempt would have been disastrous. They can argue that by the summer of 1943 Allied air supremacy had not yet been established, and Doenitz's major U-boat campaign had actually reached its climax in the Battle of the Atlantic by the March of that year (see p. 48). On the ground the Germans had about forty-one divisions in the west and, as Alan Clark pointed out in a letter to *The Times* in April 1980, Guderian had built up a strategic reserve of five Panzer divisions, three SS and the Gross Deutschland division, none of which seemed likely to be drawn into the Russian front in June 1943. Such a reserve available to German commanders in the west could well have been decisive. The Normandy landing, when it came in 1944, was in its early days a close-run thing and Brooke's fears were by no means unrealistic. From this point of view the Allies did not drift aimlessly into a Mediterranean strategy; they achieved a dispersing of enemy forces which Brooke regarded as essential if the 1944 invasion was to succeed, thereby avoiding an attempt in 1943 whose failure could well have had the most dramatic consequences (see p. 79).

# 12   Diplomacy and the question of surrender

The surrenders that did not take place during the war were as important as those that did. It has been seen how Churchill's refusal to contemplate such a course in 1940 had immensely complicated Hitler's plans (**57**). Another area where the western allies constantly feared a compromise peace, if not outright surrender, was on the Russian-German front. Since June 1941 the plains of Russia had become the major killing ground and it was vital for the west that a large part of the German army should continue to be held down there; hence the alarm in 1941 and 1942 that Russia might succumb to the strength of the German offensives; and hence, after Stalingrad, the fear that she might make a separate peace, suspecting that the west were going to let her fight alone in the hope that she and Germany might wear themselves out in war. Thus the second front, which the Russians were constantly demanding, was a delicate issue and when it did not appear immediately feasible, the west had constantly to stress the significance of the bombing offensive, the Murmansk supply convoys and the landings in North-West Africa. It was for the same reason that Churchill insisted on flying to Moscow himself to tell Stalin that there could be no second front in 1942 [**doc. 9**]. Even so, when the continuation of the Mediterranean strategy ultimately ruled this out for 1943 as well, Stalin in his annoyance recalled his ambassadors from London and Washington. The tension was made worse by the fact that the west would not recognise Russia's 1941 frontier for any post-war settlement, since that would give her Finnish Karelia, the Baltic states and eastern Poland. Indeed, after Stalingrad relations were so bad that in December 1942 and in the summer and autumn of the next year Russia did put out a cautious peace feeler through Stockholm; and in June 1943 Molotov actually had a meeting with the German Foreign Minister, Ribbentrop, at Kirovograd to consider possible terms (**11**). It is hard to know, however, how serious these moves were; they may simply have been another means of bringing the west to heel. In any case, the Germans demanded that the

Russians should pull their frontier back as far east as the Dnieper and the Russians would not accept this; so Brooke may well have been right in maintaining that the continuation of the Mediterranean campaign did not really risk closing down the Russian front.

The most controversial aspect of surrender appeared at Casablanca on 24 January 1943, when at a press conference Roosevelt officially formulated the demand that Germany, Italy and Japan would have to submit to unconditional surrender [**doc. 12**]. There were two fairly valid reasons for such a policy. One was the need to persuade the Russians that the west would not make a separate compromise peace – at a time when the plans for a continuation of the Mediterranean strategy seemed likely to preclude a cross-Channel invasion in 1943. Another was a desire to avoid the haggling and accusations of bad faith to which confusion over the Fourteen Points and the armistice agreement in 1918 had led.

Later, Roosevelt declared that his statement was purely spontaneous and Churchill in his memoirs claimed to have been taken by surprise by it (**36**). In fact, American officials had been discussing such a formula since the previous May; Churchill, six days before the press conference, had proposed that the war should continue until the unconditional surrender of Germany and Japan had been brought about, but had hoped to exclude Italy from the demand, since this might encourage her to make a separate peace. His war cabinet colleagues in London, however, who were signalled for their consent, declared that Italy should be included. The unreliability of the political leaders' memories may have been due to later doubts about the wisdom of such a demand. Equally, with so many more important questions to resolve at the time, they may have genuinely forgotten. Or it may be that Churchill's surprise arose purely over the making of the matter public.

At any rate, the notion of unconditional surrender has been strongly criticised on a number of grounds. It is thought to have caused great delay at the time of the fall of Mussolini, with the result that the Germans were able to carry out an occupation of Italy before Badoglio's government had negotiated a surrender [**doc. 13**]. Certainly it is true that although Mussolini had been placed under arrest on 25 July 1943, an Italian statement of surrender was not broadcast until 8 September – and then under some pressure. This delay, however, was partly due to the difficulty that the new Italian government found in initiating negotiations without the Germans knowing. The British and American Ministers in the Vatican had no code that had not been broken by the Germans and consequently Italian emissaries had to make a long journey to Lisbon and Tangier. It would in any case be particularly inappropriate to blame unconditional surrender for the delay, since a good deal of the time was actually taken up in discussing conditions. Unconditional surrender only made sense in a defeated country that had been totally overrun, and if the hope was to switch Italy round to the side of the Allies, conditions of some sort were inescapable, whatever the Allies may have originally demanded.

The main criticism of unconditional surrender, however, relates to Germany, and Chester Wilmot, Liddell Hart and Major General Fuller have all considered that it placed the German people in an impossible position. 'The mass of Germans', wrote Wilmot, 'saw defeat and ruin at the end of the road down which they were being marched, but none could turn off it. To the one side was the barbed wire of Nazi control; to the other the blank wall of the Allied demand for unconditional surrender' (**15**). All these writers consider, therefore, that the demand brought about an unnecessary prolongation of the war that ultimately put Russia in such a strong position in eastern Europe.

None of the critics claim that any negotiation with Hitler could be acceptable; they merely state that without this demand there would have been a greater likelihood of a *coup* which would have ended the Nazi control of Germany and have facilitated negotiations with the west. In fact, the demand for unconditional surrender did not prevent several plots before the unsuccessful attempt in July 1944, and these failures would seem to have been due purely to the great difficulty of assassinating Hitler, which was the essential feature in any change of regime. This was the core of the matter. The Germans could not turn off the road that Wilmot describes, simply because Hitler was too well entrenched. On the face of it unconditional surrender may not sound a very intelligent demand, It is, however, difficult to see that it made any difference at all.

The Morgenthau plan would seem more likely to have deterred the Germans from making peace. Henry J. Morgenthau Junior, the American Secretary of the Treasury, had proposed that after the war Germany should be broken up, her industry destroyed and her economy reduced to a simple agricultural one, and there was some embarrassment when in September 1944 these suggestions appeared in the American press. The fact that Morgenthau was a Jew made it easy for Goebbels to convince the German public that the scheme might mean what it said, and certainly any

German would feel now that the only course was to fight on to the end. On the other hand, it is doubtful whether this alone was decisive. After July 1944 Hitler had the country in his grip as never before, and the more immediate danger from the advance of the Red Army created such a desperate sense of cohesion that even if there had been no Morgenthau plan, any earlier end to the war would have been unlikely.

The 1944 plot marks the most serious attempt to bring about a change of regime, and it is tantalising to speculate on what might have happened if Hitler had not survived the bomb blast. The main purpose of the conspirators was to bring the war to an end, and at the same time to divide the Allies. A few wished to open negotiations with the Russians, but the majority preferred the west. This would have meant that five days before the beginning of General Bradley's offensive that led to the break-out in the west of Normandy, the Germans might have been prepared to open their front to the Americans and the British. Negotiations, however, would certainly have been protracted, and the Allies might have wished to strengthen their position by still embarking on the offensive. On the other hand, the new leadership in Germany would certainly have hoped to pull the line back at least as far as the Seine, from where negotiations could have continued.

If the western Allies had been prepared to make a separate deal with a new German government, German forces, which were still numerous in Normandy, could have been dispatched eastwards. After the destruction of the German Army Group Centre and the July offensive from the south of the Pripet marshes (see p. 35), the Russians had cleared the invader from their own soil and by the beginning of August had reached the Vistula. Of course, if the Allies in their suspicion of an incompletely defeated Germany had wished to make Russia a party to the settlement, then Russia would have insisted on occupying a region of Germany. If that had been accepted, then the position in eastern Europe might not have been so different from what it is today.

It is much more likely, however, that the Germans would not have agreed to this; fighting on the eastern front would have continued and it is open to question how far a newly-installed German government would have been able to cope with this, at the same time as rooting out the substantial remains of Nazi power. On the other hand, the Russians might have decided not to go on fighting alone and to have settled for a peace which brought them up to the Vistula rather than the Elbe.

# Part Four:   Assessment

Within the first year of the war Hitler's victories had brought astonishing gains. After June 1940 he controlled the Continent from the Pyrenees to half-way across Poland; Italy was his ally and he had an effective working arrangement with Russia. No man had held such power in Europe since Napoleon at Tilsit, and thus the essential question that must concern the student of the Second World War is why he should ever have lost it.

Naturally, when the explanation is narrowed down to particular items like the development of certain weapons or the outcome of certain engagements, there are many contenders on the Allied side whose claims often reflect the rivalry between the various arms of the services. In terms of global strategy, however, there are perhaps three major factors that may be singled out to explain his defeat: first, Hitler's inability to escape from a war in the west, even though his principal interest lay in the east; second, his calculated risk of a war on two fronts, when he opened his attack on Russia in the belief that she could be knocked out in one short season of *Blitzkrieg*; and third, his declaration of war on the United States immediately after the Japanese attack on Pearl Harbour.

With regard to the first factor the two most significant events of the first year of the war happened before it broke out. First, on 23 August 1939 Ribbentrop and Molotov signed the non-aggression pact which in a secret protocol ensured a fourth partition of Poland. This convinced Hitler that the west would now refuse to stand by Poland. The second significant event of that month should have warned him that he was likely to be disappointed. On 25 August the British government defied this latest move by finally signing an Anglo-Polish treaty of mutual defence, and after the German army had swept into Poland on 1 September, a declaration of war by Great Britain and France on Germany followed two days later. Thus, while *Blitzkrieg* and the Molotov-Ribbentrop pact brought about the defeat of Poland, they had also galvanised the west into a desperate and unavailing response, thereby confronting Hitler with what one of his German biographers has called 'the wrong war' (**57**).

It was always clear to Hitler that the war with the west, to which the invasion of Poland had committed him, was something of an aberration. 'Everything I undertake is aimed at Russia', he said to Carl Burckhardt, the League of Nations commissioner at Danzig, in August 1939. 'If the west is too stupid and too blind to see this, I shall be forced to come to an understanding with the Russians, defeat the west and then marshal my forces against the Soviet Union' (**87**). Thus his intention was to take on his enemies one at a time, but the problem was that as long as Great Britain continued the struggle after 1940, the war in the west was not finally closed down. A temporary stalemate ensued, but the state of hostility continued and during the last weeks of his life, in the Berlin bunker in 1945, Hitler, reflecting on the course of events, reckoned that the decisive factor in the war had been the incompleteness of his victory in 1940.

This, he concluded characteristically, was a consequence of the influence of the Jews on Churchill. In fact, the continuation of the war depended on more than Churchill's powerful determination, great though this was. It was made feasible by the three crucial decisions of that summer already noted (see p. 12) – Gort's to withdraw to Dunkirk, von Rundstedt's to halt the tanks at Gravelines, and the retention of an adequate force of RAF fighters in Great Britain. Later, when the German air force had failed to establish superiority during the Battle of Britain in August–September 1940, there was little likelihood of invasion that year [**doc. 2a, b**] and by then the United States had shown that they were prepared to stretch neutrality to the limit in giving aid to the British.

Afterwards, the romantic image of these times suggested that it was inevitable that Great Britain would continue the struggle, and that Churchill's personal correspondence with President Roosevelt had created a special relationship between the two countries, whereby American aid was bound to be provided. In fact, neither of these assumptions is correct. From 26 to 28 May, when the evacuation from Dunkirk still hung in the balance and the possibility of a French surrender was in the air, there was serious discussion in the Cabinet over a cautious enquiry about the terms that Hitler might offer. Churchill himself never favoured this, but those who contemplated it – Halifax, Chamberlain and Lloyd George – were politically too important to be ignored. Even after the successful evacuation finally of 338,000 British and Allied troops had allowed a greater optimism, there were those who feared that a continuation of the war would merely bring about the destruction of Europe to the advantage of Russia and of the United States; others who did consider remaining at war simply saw this as a way of ultimately gaining better terms from Hitler (**21**).

These doubts faded as it became increasingly clear that the British position was not hopeless, particularly with the promise of greater American aid. Earlier, however, it had been by no means a foregone conclusion that this aid would be forthcoming. It is true that since the Munich agreement in 1938 the Americans had been unable to remain indifferent to the balance of power on the Continent; their main naval force was in the Pacific, and the Atlantic no longer created an impregnable barrier of defence, particularly against infiltration into South America. Consequently, while Great Britain and France were in the field on the mainland of the Continent, Roosevelt had done his best to maintain supplies to them. However, the fall of France and the withdrawal of British forces across the Channel had raised positive doubts in his mind over whether the British could survive on their own; and if they could not, then clearly American efforts would be better spent in preparing the defence of the east coast of the United States.

This period of genuine uncertainty lasted until early August 1940, when Roosevelt eventually became convinced that Great Britain was worth backing as an outpost of American defence. At this point it could certainly be argued that the decisive factor had been Churchill's unrelenting defiance of Germany and his urging of Great Britain into a total war effort, even to the extent of the sinking of French warships for fear that they might be handed over to Germany. On 2 September a deal involving an exchange of British naval and air bases in the West Indies for fifty old American destroyers was signed between the two countries: '. . . these two great organizations of the English-speaking democracies, the British empire and the United States,' Churchill had said in the House of Commons a fortnight before, 'will have to be somewhat mixed up together in some of their affairs for mutual and general advantage. For my own part, looking out upon the future, I do not view the process with any misgivings.' The tone was relaxed, yet encouraging, suggesting that combined action between the two was a natural and obvious development, and indeed the acceptance of such a belief was the mainstay of his policy for pursuing the war to a victorious conclusion.

It had not always seemed natural and obvious to the participants and there had been a harsh note behind the negotiations. Churchill had not failed to point out that any subsequent British administration being forced to sue for terms would only have the British fleet as a major bargaining counter, and that sounded as much like a threat as a warning (**36**). On the British side it seemed that the United States had struck a hard bargain. The bases in Bermuda and Newfoundland were to be surrendered outright to the Americans; six others in the West Indies were on ninety-nine-year leases, and there were explicit promises by the British that in the event of peace with Germany the British fleet would not be handed over. In return the British had been given fifty destroyers, instead of the ninety-six that they said they needed, and these were so old that only thirty of them had been refitted by May 1941. It was perhaps understandable that some of those in government circles feared that the United States was taking advantage of Britain's predicament in order to weaken her position in the world.

Thus the continuation of the war in the west did not come about with the heroic simplicity that has sometimes been imagined. Nevertheless, it *did* come about and the events of the summer of 1940 were to be fundamental to the future shape of hostilities. The Americans did not withdraw to the defence of their eastern coast-line and the continued presence of the British in the war provided a base from which a counter-attack might one day be launched. There was not a great deal that Hitler could have done to prevent all this, once the evacuation from Dunkirk had been completed. The overrunning of France and the later digesting of the occupied territory absorbed the immediate energies of the Germans, and the Battle of Britain revealed some of the major difficulties affecting an invasion across the Channel that autumn. Still, in view of later events, he would clearly have been wiser during the next year to have concentrated on ending all resistance on his side of the Atlantic before embarking on anything further.

As it was, a peculiar feature of the period after the fall of France is that neither side appears to have had much idea about what to do next. Of course, Hitler held the initiative. The British could only maintain their defiance in a determination not to treat – KBO, keep bashing on, as Churchill put it, or in more dignified language to the House of Commons in June 1940: 'Hitler knows that he will have to break us in this island or lose the war.' Yet Hitler, too, was in something of a quandary over where to turn. The plans for a cross-Channel invasion were constantly being refurbished, and a landing in Eire was contemplated; but these projects always ran up against the inadequacy of German sea and air power.

One course of action had been suggested in June 1940, when the Spanish government, hoping to regain Gibraltar, seemed to favour an alliance with Germany. Hitler had not responded immediately. Had he done so, the course of the war would certainly have been different. Gibraltar might not have fallen, but the presence of enemy forces on either side of the Rock, together with German naval bases in the Canary Isles, would have made the landing in French North-West Africa virtually impossible and hence the later Mediterranean strategy would have been ruled out. In the autumn Hitler began to find the suggestion more appealing, but by this time the determination of the British to continue the war and the unofficial aid that they were receiving from the United States had caused Franco to have second thoughts. At a meeting between the two dictators at Hendaye on the Spanish border on 27 October 1940 he refused for the moment to agree to a free passage for German troops on their way to attack Gibraltar (**9**).

The day after this meeting Hitler's attention was suddenly drawn to the other end of the Mediterranean, when Mussolini launched his attack on Greece. Hitler had only heard of this plan at the last moment and would have liked to stop it. Even so, he did not immediately drop the Gibraltar scheme, and a directive on 12 November 1940 spoke of massing troops on the Spanish border. On 6 December, however, General Wavell launched the desert offensive under General O'Connor against Marshal Graziani. The rapid success of this (see p. 17) did not merely force Hitler to send troops to assist his ally – the beginning of the Afrika Korps; it demonstrated to Franco that he would be wise to give up any thought of a German alliance, and Hitler's later proposals met with a consistent refusal.

Before this Hitler's interest had already turned to an attack on Russia, an intention which he had announced as early as 29–31 July 1940 at a conference at the Berghof. This did not stop the Battle of Britain from taking place, nor affect the continuing examination of plans to invade Britain and the bombing of London throughout the winter. Yet the future Russian campaign came more and more to occupy his thoughts. This aim, which was the second major factor in his defeat, had always been an integral part of Nazi doctrine; indeed, it had a longer ancestry than that, since behind it lay a central European fear already voiced at the end of the nineteenth century that one day the Russians would have become so numerous as to be irresistible and that it was therefore important to knock them out before then. For Hitler there was also the practical consideration of the millions of tonnes of Russian wheat and oil that would be made available to Germany.

To embark on this, however, meant taking the risk that while Great Britain was still defiant and receiving increasing aid from the United States, Germany might later be faced with fighting a war on two fronts. In *Mein Kampf* Hitler had actually blamed the Kaiser for doing this, but by now the presence of Great Britain as an enemy, far from militating against an attack on Russia, became an argument for it. The British, it was thought, could only continue their resistance because they hoped ultimately for assistance from Russia and the United States. If, therefore, a swift German attack on Russia were to bring about her subordination to Germany, the British would be robbed of one potential ally, and Japan, freed from any danger from Russia, would become such a threat to the United States that the Americans would desist from aiding the British. In these circumstances it appeared unlikely that Great Britain would continue very long on her own [**doc. 3a, b**].

Furthermore, Hitler did not anticipate any danger of a diversion from the west, since he reckoned he would defeat Russia by the late autumn and it was unlikely that the British would be able to respond in that time. In fact, this was to be the end of the *Blitzkrieg* phase of the war and when the German armies were unable to bring about the rapid defeat which he had intended, the scene in Europe was transformed into a horrific war of attrition in which the vast resources of Russia were ultimately to predominate (see p. 57). And yet Hitler had not been alone in his optimism; most of his generals believed that a single season would be sufficient; and in the west British and American military thinking had assumed the likelihood of a Russian collapse. It is therefore important to consider why the Germans were unable to achieve their purpose.

One explanation has concentrated on the timing of the operation. In December 1940 Hitler ordered that all preparations for an invasion of Russia must be complete by 15 May 1941, but later this date was shifted back to 22 June. A principal reason for the delay was the short Balkan campaign whereby Hitler endeavoured to secure his right flank before venturing on the major offensive (see p. 19). After the Yugoslav revolt the rapid thrust of the German Panzers through the Balkans into Greece was a swift and successful operation. It was yet more remarkable that after such a campaign the German army could still meet its new date for the invasion of Russia on 22 June. Nevertheless, the fact remains that in the German offensive of 1941 the two great thrusts on Moscow and in the south towards the Causasus had not reached their objectives before the onset of winter.

There has consequently been considerable speculation on the significance of the Balkan campaign in bringing about a loss of several weeks, which could have been decisive. On the British side this has been put forward as a justification for the costly expedition to Greece. Equally, Hitler at the end of his life reckoned that the delay was fatal and had been caused by his own kindness in coming to the assistance of Mussolini against the Greeks (**57**).

Neither of these views is entirely correct. The British intervention does not seem to have caused any great prolongation of the Balkan campaign – except for the attack on Crete, which Hitler himself had not been keen to undertake. Hitler, too, had not been particularly governed by his friendship with Mussolini. It was the Yugoslav revolt that made a German occupation inescapable before the attack on Russia could go ahead, and the extension of this fighting into Greece was not a rescue operation for Mussolini. It was brought about by the fact that Italy was at war with Greece and obviously the British might try to take advantage of this, for example by establishing air bases there for the bombing of Romanian oil fields. Actually it was only towards the end of February 1941 that the British cabinet, after a great deal of anguished debate, decided to send military aid to Greece, but Hitler could not know of these doubts and was convinced that he must clear the mainland. Thus the postponement of the invasion of Russia may be regarded as a consequence of the Yugoslav revolt and, more indirectly, of the Italian attack on Greece in October 1940 – two decisions in which neither Hitler nor the British played much part.

In any case, it is doubtful whether the delay in the launching of the attack on Russia was the main reason for the German failure to defeat her before the end of 1941. The summer came late that year and the ground would have been too marshy for any advance into Russia during much of the time between 15 May and 22 June. In addition, some critics of Hitler's tactics have pointed out that far more time than that was lost when he switched the main effort towards the Caucasus and called off the advance on Moscow throughout August and September, when the weather was fine [**doc. 6**]. This argument assumes that the taking of Moscow by the Germans would have been decisive. From the beginning, however,

Hitler had argued quite soundly that the German aim must be to destroy the Russian armies, rather than simply to make territorial gains. Consequently it was not relevant to try to capture Moscow, since the development of an economic base east of the Urals suggests that the Russians would have continued to fight, even if their capital had fallen. And Hitler's switch to the south did bring about a successful encirclement east of Kiev, where some 600,000 Russians were caught, and if land was to be considered, the capture of the rich southern regions was not unrealistic.

So why did the German *Blitzkrieg* fail? One reason would seem to be the appalling state of the Russian roads which played havoc with the German wheeled vehicles [**doc. 5**]. This in turn must have played its part in the inability of the Germans to complete their encircling movements except at Minsk and Kiev. Thus the Red Army pulling back over the vast spaces at its disposal remained intact. It had of course suffered dreadful losses, but here the Germans encountered the real source of Russian strength – the great numbers of men who could be mobilised. German intelligence had reckoned that they would have to face 200 divisions. By August their armies had dealt with these, but were then confronted with a further 160; in December the Russian counter-attack began with 100 divisions. And behind all this seemingly limitless manpower there lay an economic potential in Siberia that remained out of the German reach.

The murderous to and fro on the Russian front was to be an appalling drain on the German army and this certainly establishes eastern Europe as the decisive theatre in the war. The significance of continuing hostilities with Great Britain is debatable for much of this period; the fighting in the North African desert consumed only a small part of the German forces; on the other hand, it was necessary for considerable numbers of German troops to remain in France, Norway and, later, in Italy, and the eventual opening of a second front was ultimately to lead to the partition of Germany. Nevertheless, when one considers the performance of the German army in western Europe in 1944 and 1945 and the hazards attending the Normandy invasion (see p. 30), it is extremely doubtful whether that second front in the west would have had a chance of success without the economic and military power of the United States.

Before December 1941 the full granting of that power was by no means assured. Some certainly was forthcoming, when from August 1940 Roosevelt had decided that Great Britain was worth backing. However, he still hoped to keep America out of the war and justified this with the argument that the United States would be free to supply far more material if she were not a belligerent. At first he was hampered by the approaching presidential election of November 1940, but once he had won a further term of office – his third – substantial forms of aid were devised. The problem for the British of meeting immediate payment was overcome in March 1941 by Lend-Lease (see p. 56), but there remained the difficulty of policing the whole extent of the Atlantic, when those goods were delivered. In July the Americans took over the occupation of Iceland, but Roosevelt still hesitated over providing escorts for the Atlantic convoys, since he was conscious of the nervousness of the American people about being drawn into the war; in September 1941, however, after an incident in which a German U-boat had fired on an American destroyer, he felt able to declare that American defensive waters extended across the Atlantic up to a point some four hundred miles west of Scotland (**21**).

By now the drift to an unofficial war-time alliance had become very marked. In June 1941 German and Italian assets had been frozen in the United States, and in August there took place a personal meeting between Churchill and Roosevelt on a battleship off Newfoundland, when the general nature of the peace aims was defined in a document to be known as the Atlantic Charter. And in November sections of the American Neutrality Act were repealed by Congress so as to allow the entry of American vessels into belligerent ports and the arming of merchant vessels. Yet at this point it was still doubtful whether the United States would fulfil Churchill's hopes and come openly into the war. The voting over the repeal of the sections of the Neutrality Act had been very close and the Democrats had not given their President total support. Indeed, Roosevelt himself may well have been hoping that it would still be sufficient for the United States to act as the arsenal of democracy, without having actually to go to war.

It was Hitler's third major strategic blunder that suddenly changed all this. He was certainly aware of the growing closeness of co-operation between the United States and Great Britain, but although it must have irritated him greatly, he had tried hard to avoid upsetting American feelings ever since his invasion of Russia. Then on 7 December 1941 Japan opened hostilities against the Americans with the attack from the air on Pearl Harbour in Hawaii and four days later this was followed by a German declaration of war on the United States.

Why did Hitler do it? It could of course be said that the German declaration merely made explicit what American actions had implied throughout the past two years. It may be that the sheer audacity of the Pearl Harbour attack excited him at a time when he was depressed over his own fortunes in Russia; or that he was obsessed with America as the supposed headquarters of international Jewry. None of this makes very much sense. Diplomatically the Anti-Comintern pact of 1936 with Japan did not commit Germany to a war against America, and the tripartite pact of September 1940 was only a treaty of mutual defence in the event of an attack from outside. It is true that on 4 December 1941 Germany had agreed to support Japan in any war that she might wage; yet the assault by the Japanese on the United States hardly suited Hitler, who would have much preferred them to attack Singapore or Russia, and he could have pleaded his own circumstances in order to avoid immediate action. Furthermore, if he had remained neutral, the war effort of the United States might have become concentrated on the Pacific. As it was, with this gesture of desperation he had at last granted Churchill what he had been hoping for since the summer of 1940 and had consolidated a Grand Alliance against Germany in a war on two fronts. From now on Germany could not win; the only question was whether she could escape outright defeat.

One of Hitler's biographers has remarked: 'in little more than two years he had gambled away a dominant political position' (**57**), and these three strategic decisions would seem to have been fundamental to Germany's undoing. Much of the criticism voiced about Hitler, however, has been aimed rather more at a tactical level. How generally damaging were Hitler's interventions in military matters? Many of his generals have been glad to make him the scapegoat for every military disaster, but in the field of tactics this would not seem to be entirely reasonable. Even though there were mistakes, he must also receive credit for a good deal. He adopted the technique of *Blitzkrieg* and seized on the Manstein plan in 1940, when the more orthodox of his generals were doubtful about it. In his desire to gain the Caucasus in 1942 (see p. 25), in the Mortain counter-attack in 1944 (see p. 35), and in his determination to protect the Ruhr in the last winter of the war (see p. 38), the general concept was not unsound; the weakness lay in his apparent ignorance of the immense preponderance of the Allies in the air and on the ground, a consequence of his remaining shut away in the unreal atmosphere of his headquarters, unlike Churchill who went everywhere.

There are other charges which are more difficult to answer. He was certainly responsible for the outcome of the German offensive in the summer of 1942, when his obsession with the capture of Stalingrad caused him to neglect his main objective in the Caucasus and to leave his long northern flank inadequately guarded [**doc. 10**]. And after the Allied landings in Morocco and Algeria he should not have poured so many men into Tunisia, where they were bound to be lost – as Rommel warned him. The main criticism centres on his constant refusal to allow any withdrawal to a more effective defence line. Rommel's own tactics in the desert had already shown how a tactical withdrawal might be the necessary prelude to an advance, and similar tactics in Russia and France, so often requested by his generals, might have enabled them to fight a more successful campaign there, although it is impossible to know how long their alternative defence lines would have held. It seems to be generally conceded, however, that his determination to hold his ground in Russia during the winter of 1941 was probably the correct course, since withdrawal then might well have turned into a headlong flight under pressure of the Russian attack (**74**).

The most intriguing aspect of Hitler's contribution to the course of the war is to be found in the Normandy campaign. Unlike his generals, he did guess correctly that the Allied invasion would be on the Normandy coast, not by intuition, but by a series of shrewd calculations that they could well have made for themselves. And his support of Rommel's plan to destroy the invasion on the beaches suggests that he understood better how to deal with it than others did. Yet he did not act on this. Why not? Partly because of his obsessive mistrust of the men who served him. As a result, Rommel only had one division in reserve under his direct command and the rest were held too far back and under the control of supreme headquarters. But he was also unfortunate in that the one occasion when he was cautious about Allied strength was in the summer of 1944, when he relied upon an exaggerated assessment by his staff officers. As a result, he became convinced that the Allies still had many more troops in England than they had actually landed in Normandy and this led to his being deluded by the deception plan (see p. 31).

If the main opportunity for driving the Allies into the sea had been missed, the other hope for the Germans was to seal off the invasion area and to force the Allies to a stalemate, but the sheer bulk of men and material that the Allies could ferry into the bridgehead made this unlikely. It might have been possible to prepare a further defence line well in the rear along the Seine, as Rommel and others had suggested, but Hitler would not hear of this and as a consequence, when the Allies did break out, the subsequent retreat was to take the Germans right out of France. On the other hand, if the Normandy line had not held, would an improvised line on the Seine have served any better?

What is clear is that the summer of 1944 was the key to the eventual outcome of the war. The Allies had taken great care over the invasion, but success had still hung on a number of unpredictable factors and the balance between great victory and disaster or stalemate was very fine. The Allies could have been pushed back into the sea in June 1944, and it would probably have taken two years for any further attempt to be launched. What would have happened in the meantime? Would American disillusionment have led the United States to turn back to concentrate on the Pacific front? Would despair in the west have brought about the fall of Churchill's government and a compromise peace? Or, if the war had continued in the absence of a western invasion force, would the Russian advance have eventually taken the Red Army to the Rhine rather than the Elbe? Or would the Germans, freed from an immediate commitment in the west, have been able to halt the Russian advance?

All these questions became a matter of conjecture, once the Allies were beating up against the western border of Germany. What mattered now was the manner in which they would link up with the Russians and here the decisive factor was the astonishing ability of the Germans to continue to resist. In France they had lost more than 300,000 men and had been forced back as far as the Dutch border; on the eastern front the destruction of Army Group Centre had cost them another 300,000 men and the Russian advance had brought the Red Army to the Vistula; in Italy the Allies had reached 160 kilometres north of Rome. Yet a frantic building of new units eventually enabled the Germans to put up an extremely tough defence which did not succumb until the spring of 1945.

These additional six or seven months of fighting were to have a striking effect upon the post-war map of Europe, for it was in that time that the Red Army overran most Balkan countries, eventually broke into eastern Europe and Berlin, and presented Stalin with a position from which he could gain most of his demands at the Yalta conference in February 1945. 'What, with the possible of exception of the Kuriles,' asked Edward Stettinius, the American Secretary of State, 'did the Soviet Union receive at Yalta which she might not have taken without any agreement?'

In a book written shortly after the beginning of the cold war it was perhaps natural that Chester Wilmot should imply sinister motives to most of Stalin's moves at this time – the great left-flanking sweep along the line of the Danube to gain the Balkan countries, the refusal to aid the Poles who rose in revolt in Warsaw in August 1944 and who were then massacred by the Germans, and the encouragement given to the west to make a landing in the south of France, instead of thrusting north-east from Italy into Churchill's 'soft underbelly of the Axis', where their forces might have forestalled the Red Army (**15**).

In fact, more recent reflection on these developments has suggested that the motives were military rather than political. The pause made by the Russians on the Vistula was largely dictated by the need for supplies to catch up after the great advance against the German Army Group Centre, and the firmer resistance on the border of Germany made a left-flanking movement along the Danube easier to carry out. It could well be that the Russians were not averse to seeing a non-Communist Polish resistance wiped out by the Germans, but they have also argued that, since the general shape of the Russian advance did not require the capture of Warsaw, Rokossovski intended to bypass it and the Russian high command was not going to be deflected from this by any Polish rising. And the landings in the south of France were largely as the Americans had wished, since they would complete the liberation of France and provide the Allies with a badly needed port in Marseilles. There were, of course, arguments against the landings – as being unnecessary, because Allied success in the north would in any case compel the Germans to pull out; and too costly, because the removal of forces from General Alexander for the operation was bound to slow down his own advance in Italy. But even those who had felt these doubts had never favoured a campaign in the Balkans, where the terrain was ideally suited for defence.

The only thing that could have affected the eventual outcome was an Anglo-American military victory in the west, ending the war in the autumn of 1944. This possibility lies behind the great controversy over the narrow and the broad front (see p. 36).

Montgomery was the main protagonist of the narrow front, which characteristically was also going to be *his* front. He envisaged an immense concentration of Allied power keeping up the momentum of the pursuit into the Low Countries, punching a way across the river barriers of the Meuse and the Rhine, thereby avoiding the Siegfried Line and capturing the Ruhr, without which Germany could not hope to continue the war. As General Blumentritt said afterwards, 'he who holds northern Germany holds Germany', and German generals were virtually unanimous in their belief that a continuing thrust by the Allies in September could have met with only minor resistance. 'The sudden penetration of the British Task forces into Antwerp (4 September) took the Fuhrer's headquarters utterly by surprise', said General Student. 'At that moment we had no disposable reserves worth mentioning either on the western front or within our own country' [**doc. 14**].

The Americans were also advocating a concerted thrust, but further south by their own Twelfth Army Group, whose Third Army under General Patton was driving hard for the Saar and was only 160 kilometres from the Rhine. Eisenhower's compromise, allowing the British and the American Army Groups each to have its offensive in turn, meant in effect that the Allied line was still to advance eastwards on a broad front. In the event neither offensive was successful, and during the lull following these setbacks the Germans were able to reorganise sufficiently to continue the fight into 1945.

Eisenhower's principal reason for making this decision was logistic. The supply of his forces depended very largely on road transport coming all the way from Cherbourg, since most of the Channel ports were holding out in a state of siege. The landings in the south of France had given the Allies the use of Marseilles as a port, but this too was a long way from the northern area where Montgomery proposed to operate. In these precarious circumstances Eisenhower was convinced that he should consolidate on a broad front the immense territorial gains that had been made, before embarking on new adventures.

The fate of the Arnhem operation may bear this view out, since Montgomery's problem did not derive from any excessive diverting of supplies to Patton, who was receiving very little, but from the fact that Antwerp, although captured by the British, could not be used as a port for a further eighty-three days, while the estuary of the Scheldt was still in the hands of the Germans.

Tactically the venture had suffered from great misfortunes – bad weather had delayed many of the airborne operations; the single road linking the landing points was too narrow to make an effective axis for the breakthrough by an armoured division; it so happened that 9 SS Panzer Division was stationed to the north of Arnhem and two excellent German commanders, Student and Model, were both immediately on the spot. At best, the operation had been a magnificently brave shot, but without Arnhem the territory gained was a meaningless salient (**85**).

In all, one cannot say for certain how easily the war might have been concluded by the autumn of 1944. The later performance of the German army would suggest that German generals may afterwards have exaggerated the extent to which an opportunity was lost; it would no doubt appeal to them to blame Allied military incompetence for the occupation of eastern Germany by the Red Army, and it never seemed to occur to them that the outcome was largely the consequence of their own successful military defence in the west. Montgomery's plan in principle could have been right, but in practice the problem of supply may have been decisive. Certainly the Scheldt should have been cleared before the Arnhem operation was launched, but by then it might have been too late. In Sir Basil Liddell Hart's view the best chance of winning in that autumn was lost when Patton's tanks ran out of petrol, after reaching the Meuse at the end of August, as a result of Eisenhower's compromise agreement with Montgomery (**11**). All this, however, must remain a matter of speculation. The advance from the beaches of Normandy had been swift and extensive, and it may be that the circumstances of the autumn of 1944 were simply the result of the lull that usually imposes itself after an offensive has run its course.

The Anglo-American advance was slowed down still further by Hitler's determination to mount the Ardennes counter-attack against the west, and although this was checked, it naturally set back the timing of any offensive intended by the Allies. More particularly, when Hitler finally called off further attack early in January, he had exhausted his last reserves. This meant that he was unable to cope with the new offensive launched by the Russians on 12 January from the front which they had established in Poland the previous summer, and by early February the westernmost units of the Red Army had reached Kuestrin on the Oder only 80 kilometres east of Berlin (**82, 84**).

At the same time the remaining German forces in the Rhineland had orders to fight on the west side of the Rhine (see p. 38). This continued resistance in the west, combined with the Ardennes counter-attack, was all part of a desperate political gamble by Hitler that the British and Americans, alarmed by the Soviet advance, would end their alliance with Russia. 'They had not counted on our defending ourselves step by step and holding them off in the west like madmen, while the Russians drive deeper and deeper into Germany', said Goering at the end of January (**15**). But the alliance held firm and the only consequence of Hitler's policy was that at a time when the future borders and regimes of eastern Europe were all in the making, it was not until late in March that the Anglo-American forces succeeded in crossing the Rhine.

The Americans, however, did reach the Elbe on 11 April and were some 110 kilometres from Berlin five days before the Russians launched their final attack from the Oder. Churchill, too, was hoping that Montgomery's Army Group driving north-east could make a rush to get to Berlin first. Equally, by the beginning of May, Patton was on the borders of Czechoslovakia and could certainly have been the first to take Prague. But President Roosevelt, before his death on 12 April, had already set his seal on the last stages of the war. He believed that he had a good working arrangement with Stalin and hoped for his aid against Japan. Accordingly, the American government preferred to avoid any possible clash and left Berlin and Prague to the Russians. In any case, Eisenhower was determined that military movements should not be sullied by political considerations, and his main concern was to concentrate his forces southwards against the National Redoubt, where it was imagined that die-hard Nazis would conduct a last fanatical stand. In fact, the National Redoubt did not exist and the only outcome was that the Red Army gained two more European capitals.

War is a strange and deadly combination of rational calculation and mad chance. Sometimes that chance lies outside human control; the future of nations was decided by the state of the weather in the Channel at the end of May 1940 and again in June 1944; also by the failure of the conspirators' bomb in July 1944. Sometimes human efforts will produce results contrary to all reasonable expectations, and a ferocious patriotism will sustain a defence beyond the point when it is apparently possible. It was this, for example, that frustrated the German attack on the Russians in 1941 and 1942, although this still might not have

83

sufficed if the Russians had had a decent system of roads that the Germans could have used. There was a similar desperate determination in the continuing German resistance in the west after the Battle of Normandy. Equally, in the political field it was, on the face of it, an understandable decision of the French to make peace in June 1940, and hardly to be expected that the British would carry on alone afterwards. At least, Hitler found it puzzling.

The balance between the rational and the apparently irrational can be best appreciated in the field of tactics. Here the weakness of orthodoxy is that it becomes predictable, and occasionally some insight into new possibilities will give the advantage to the unorthodox. The Germans should not have been able to break through in the Ardennes in May 1940; technically the French staff were right to assume that Guderian could not cross the Meuse in a single day (**70**). O'Connor should not have driven point-blank at Graziani's enormously greater forces in the desert in December 1940, and Rommel should not have been able to drive him back with the aid of dummy tanks. And yet, although the unorthodox will sometimes win, it cannot always – and seldom in the long term – since the weakness of the unorthodox is that it ignores the teaching of experience. Charles XII of Sweden won the battle of Narva against extraordinary odds, but he lost the Northern War – and deserved to do so. And Hitler, although he had a remarkable political and military flair, deserved to lose his, too.

There are many reasons that help to explain the defeat of Germany – the total destruction of German air power, the inability positively to command the sea, and the enormous advantage of Ultra for the Allies. The two greatest are probably the economic potential of the United States, coupled with the working relationship between Churchill and Roosevelt, and the vast sources of manpower available to the Red Army in those long desperate campaigns across the plains of Russia. These last two, however, could have played little part, if Hitler had not brought on himself the Grand Alliance of Great Britain, the United States and Russia, thus driving his country into war on two fronts, the great mistake of 1914, which he had criticised in *Mein Kampf*. Long before the end, it was clear that the only hope for Germany was to separate the west from Russia, the aim common to Hitler and the conspirators of 20 July 1944, and eventually Hitler's propaganda concentrated on little else [**doc. 15**]. During the war, this was not to be. The break only came afterwards with the Cold War, and soon proved its significance in the relatively rapid rehabilitation of West Germany.

Even so, the German performance in wartime was truly remarkable. One historian, H. Trevor-Roper, has commented: 'What nearly won the war was German industry and the German army, which in its early days, the days of its political skill, the dictatorship did indeed foster and serve.' The German army was able to hold off the fury of the vast masses of Soviet Russia for four years, at the same time as conducting a defence in the west sufficiently effective to make an Anglo-American invasion an extremely hazardous operation. And when the retreat had taken them as far back as the Netherlands, their resilience was such that the Allies could not break through across the Rhine until the spring of 1945, and by that time the Red Army was close to Berlin. It is thus an irony of history that the eventual Soviet hold on east Germany, Poland and the Balkans should have been the consequence of the extraordinary quality of the German army in resisting the onslaught of its enemies from the west.

# Part Five: Documents

## The conception of *Blitzkrieg*

**(a)** *The swiftness of the German victories in the first year of the war was largely due to the practice of* Blitzkrieg. *One of the principal exponents of this technique was General Guderian, whose Panzer Corps of three divisions swept through the Ardennes and crossed the Meuse on 13 May 1940. It was ironical that much of this new theory had been thought out during the inter-war years by a British military commentator, Basil Liddell Hart, as Guderian admitted in his memoirs (see p. 4).*

It was principally the books and articles of the Englishmen, Fuller, Liddell Hart and Martel, that excited my interest and gave me food for thought. These far-sighted soldiers were even then trying to make of the tank something more than just an infantry support weapon. They envisaged it in relationship to the growing motorization of our age, and thus they became the pioneers of a new type of warfare on the largest scale.

I learned from them the concentration of armour, as employed in the battle of Cambrai. Further, it was Liddell Hart who emphasised the use of armoured forces for long-range strokes, operations against the opposing army's communications, and also proposed a type of armoured division combining Panzer and Panzer-infantry units. Deeply impressed by these ideas, I tried to develop them in a sense practicable for our own army. So I owe many suggestions of our further development to Captain Liddell Hart.

Guderian, H., *Panzer Leader* (**48**), p. 20.

**(b)** *The irony of this was also emphasised in Liddell Hart's own memoirs.*

The collapse of the west in 1940 was a world-shaking disaster which changed the course of history for the worse. Yet never was a great disaster more easily preventable.

The Panzer forces' thrust could have been stopped long before reaching the Channel by a concentrated counterstroke with similar forces. But the French, though having more and better tanks than the enemy, had strung them out in small packets in the 1918 way. The one British armoured division was not despatched to France until after the German offensive was launched, and thus arrived too late for the first, and decisive, phase.

The thrust could have been stopped earlier, on the Meuse, if the French had not rushed into Belgium leaving their hinge so weak, or had moved reserves there sooner. For the French Command had not only regarded the Ardennes as impassable to tanks, but reckoned that any attack on the Meuse would be a set-piece assault in the 1918 style and could not be delivered before the ninth day of the offensive because of the time required for preparation after arrival on the Meuse – thus allowing the French Command ample time to bring up its reserves. But Guderian's Panzer Corps, reaching the river early on 13 May, stormed the crossings that same afternoon (the fourth day). A 'tank-time' pace of action bowled over an out of date 'slow-motion'.

But this *Blitzkrieg* pace was only possible because the Allied leaders had not grasped the new technique, and so did not know how to counter it. The thrust could have been stopped before it even reached the Meuse, if the approaches had been well covered with minefields. It could have been stopped even if mines were lacking – by the simple expedient of felling the trees along the forest roads which led to the Meuse. The loss of time in clearing them would have been fatal to the German chances. For the issue turned on the time-factor.

. . . As Guderian stated, in his war memoirs and elsewhere, that he owed his success largely to applying my ideas of tank strategy and tactics – describing himself as my 'disciple and pupil' – I have particularly good reason to gauge how this fatal thrust could have been checked. Having thought out the new method of attack in the nineteen-twenties, it did not require any great effort to discover the antidote well before 1940. It was hard, however, to get it understood by generals who were still thinking in terms of 1918. By 1942 all armies had learned how to check a *Blitzkrieg* attack – but a lot would have been saved if Hitler's opponents had learned before the war.

For me, in that Spring of 1940, there was a tragic irony in having to watch, as a mere onlooker, my ideas being applied to pierce the defence of France, my birthplace, and put in extreme jeopardy my own country.

Liddell Hart, B. H., *Memoirs*, Vol 2., Cassell, 1965, pp. 280–81.

**document 2**

## British prospects in the summer of 1940

**(a)** *As the battle in Belgium and France developed in May 1940, Winston Churchill asked his chiefs of staff to give a reasoned assessment of Great Britain's ability to continue the war alone in the event of a French surrender. The report that they submitted was signed by all three chiefs of staff and their vice-chiefs.*

2. Our conclusions are contained in the following paragraphs:

3. While our Air Force is in being, our Navy and Air Force together should be able to prevent Germany carrying out a serious sea-borne invasion of this country.

4. Supposing Germany gained complete air superiority, we consider that the Navy could hold up an invasion for a time, but not for an indefinite period.

5. If, with our Navy unable to prevent it, and our Air Force gone, Germany attempted an invasion, our coast and beach defences could not prevent the German tanks and infantry getting a firm footing on our shores. In the circumstances envisaged above, our land forces would be insufficient to deal with a serious invasion.

6. The crux of the matter is air superiority. Once Germany had attained this, she might attempt to subjugate this country by air attack alone.

7. Germany could not gain complete air superiority, unless she could knock out our Air Force and the aircraft industries, some vital portions of which are concentrated at Coventry and Birmingham.

8. Air attacks on the aircraft factories would be made by day or by night. We consider that we should be able to inflict such casualties on the enemy by day as to prevent serious damage. Whatever we do, however, by way of defensive measures – and we are pressing on with these with all dispatch – we cannot be sure of protecting the large industrial centres, upon which our aircraft industries depend, from serious material damage by night attack. The enemy would not have to employ precision bombing to achieve this effect.

9. Whether the attacks succeed in eliminating the aircraft industry depends not only on the material damage by bombs, but on the moral effect on the work people and their determination to carry on in the face of wholesale havoc and destruction.

10. If, therefore, the enemy presses home night attacks on our

aircraft industry, he is likely to achieve such material and moral damage within the industrial area concerned as to bring all work to a standstill.

11. It must be remembered that numerically the Germans have a superiority of four to one. Moreover, the German aircraft factories are well dispersed and relatively inaccessible.

12. On the other hand, so long as we have a counter-offensive bomber force, we can carry out similar attacks on German industrial centres and by moral and material effect bring a proportion of them to a standstill.

13. To sum up, our conclusion is that *prima facie* Germany has most of the cards; but the real test is whether the morale of our fighting personnel and civil population will counterbalance the numerical and material advantages which Germany enjoys. We believe it will.

Churchill, W. S., *History of the Second World War* (**36**), Vol. 2, pp. 78–9.

(**b**) *In the summer of 1945 Liddell Hart was able to interview many of the German generals shortly after their capture, and their views confirmed the uncertainties that attended the prospect of invading Great Britain in 1940 (see p. 15).*

Rundstedt: "The responsibility of commanding the invasion fell to me, and the task was assigned to my Army Corps. The 16th Army under General Busch was on the right and the 9th Army under General Strauss was on the left. They were to sail from ports stretching from Holland to Le Havre" . . . Rundstedt indicated on the map the sector over which the landings were to be made from Dover to near Portsmouth. "We were then to push forward and establish a much larger bridgehead along an arc south of London. It ran up the south shore of the Thames to the outskirts of London and then south-westwards to Southampton Water."

General Siewert: "Our idea was to finish the war as quickly as possible and we *had* to get across the water to do that." "Then why wasn't it carried out?" I asked. "There were many preparations in progress, but the weather outlook was not good. The attempt was supposed to be carried out in September, but Hitler cancelled all the preparations, because he thought it impracticable. The Navy's heart was not in it, and it was not strong enough to protect the flanks. Neither was the German Air Force strong enough to stop the British Navy."

Liddell Hart, B. H., *The Other Side of the Hill* (**54**), pp. 218–19.

**document 3**
# The conception of the attack on Russia

**(a)** *The initial enthusiasm. These extracts from General Halder's diary demonstrate the German belief that Russia must be removed as a possible ally for the British (see p. 73).*

*13 July 1940*

The Fuehrer is very much preoccupied with the problem of why England does not wish to come to terms. He sees the answer, as we do, in the fact that England still has some hopes of Russia. He therefore expects that he will have to compel her by force to make peace. But he is reluctant to do this. Reason: if we crush England by force of arms, the British Empire will fall to pieces. But that would be of no advantage to Germany. We should spill German blood only in order that Japan, America and others might benefit.

*31 July 1940*

Something must have happened in London. The English were down and out; now their spirits have revived again. (We know from) intercepted conversations (that) Russia has been unpleasantly affected by the rapid development of the situation in the west. She need only suggest to England that she does not want to see a strong Germany and the English, like drowning men, will clutch at the hope that within six or eight months the situation will be transformed. With Russia defeated, England's last hope is blotted out and then Germany becomes master of Europe and the Balkans.

Decision: *We must settle accounts with Russia and destroy her in the spring of 1941.*

*The quicker Russia is smashed the better. The operation only makes sense if we shatter the Russian state at a single blow.* To gain tracts of territory is not enough. To stand still in winter is dangerous. Therefore it is better to wait, but with the firm resolve to finish Russia off. This is also necessary on account of the situation in the Baltic. Two great states cannot co-exist there side by side. May 1941: operations would take five months to complete. Much better if it were possible this year; but that would not be practicable as a concerted operation.

**(b)** *Second thoughts.*

*Halder's diary: 28 January 1941*
The objectives are not clear. We do not strike at England and our own economic potential will not be improved. We ought not to underestimate the threat from the west. It may be that Italy will collapse, following the loss of her colonies, and that we shall be caught up in a southern front in Spain, Italy and Greece. If we are then committed to an attack on Russia, our position will become more difficult.

*von Weizsaecker, Secretary of State, to Ribbentrop: April 1941*
I can summarize in one sentence my views on a German-Russian conflict. If every Russian city reduced to ashes were as valuable to us as a sunken British warship, I should advocate an attack on Russia this summer. As it is, I believe that our victory in Russia would be purely military; in an economic sense we should come off the losers.

It may perhaps be considered an attractive prospect to give the Communist system its death blow. To rally the whole Eurasian continent against the Anglo-Saxons and their following may also seem consistent with the logic of events. But the only decisive factor is whether this plan will hasten the defeat of England. We must distinguish between two possibilities:

(a) England is about to collapse. If we accept this, we shall encourage her by taking on a new opponent. Russia is not a natural ally of England, who can expect nothing good from her. It is not belief in Russia which is preserving England from collapse
. . .

(b) We do not believe in the imminent collapse of England. It may be argued that we must feed ourselves by force from Soviet territory. While I take it for granted that we should advance victoriously to Moscow and beyond, I doubt very much whether we should be able to exploit what we have gained in face of the notorious passive resistance of the Slavs. I see in Russia no effective opposition to the Communist system which we could use or with which we could make common cause. We should therefore have to reckon, most probably, with a survival of Stalin's system in Eastern Russia and Siberia and with a renewal of hostilities in the spring of 1942. Our window on the Pacific would remain closed.

All extracts quoted in Gwyer, J. M. A., *Grand Strategy* (**1b**), Vol 3, Part 1, pp. 50, 52, 73–4.

**document 4**
# The directive for the German attack on Russia

*This was issued on 18 December 1940 and at that date envisaged an opening of operations by 15 May 1941 (see p. 20 and p. 73).*

The armed forces of Germany must be prepared, even before the conclusion of the war with England, *to defeat Soviet Russia* in *one rapid campaign* (Operation Barbarossa.).

The Army must in this case be prepared to commit all available formations, with the proviso that the occupied territories must be secured against surprise attacks.

The Air Force will have to make available for the support of the army in the Eastern Campaign forces of adequate strength to ensure a rapid termination to the land action and to give the East German territories maximum protection against enemy air raids. This making of the main effort in the East must not be carried to a point at which we can no longer adequately protect the totality of our battle and our armament zones against enemy air attacks, nor must the offensive against England, and in particular against England's supply routes, suffer in consequence.

For the Navy the point of main effort will remain consistently against England, even while the Eastern Campaign is in progress. I [Hitler] shall give the order for the assembly of troops etc. for the proposed operation against Soviet Russia, should the occasion arise, eight weeks before the operation is due to begin.

Preparations that require more time than this shall – so far as they have not already been made – be begun at once and are to be completed by 15 May 1941.

Great stress, however, must be laid on disguising any offensive intentions.

Preparations by the High Commands are to be based on the following considerations:

1. General intention

The mass of the army stationed in western Russia is to be destroyed in bold operations involving deep penetrations by armoured spearheads, and the withdrawal of elements capable of combat into the extensive land spaces is to be prevented.

By means of a rapid pursuit a line is then to be reached from beyond which the Russian air force will no longer be capable of attacking the German home territories. The final objective of the operation is to be the attainment of a line sealing off Asiatic Russia and running, in general, the Volga-Archangel. From such a line the one remaining Russian industrial area in the Urals can be eliminated by the air force, should the need arise . . .

Guderian, H., *Panzer Leader* (**48**), pp. 513–14.

## German difficulties in Russia

**document 5**

*In the summer of 1945 three German generals, von Kleist, von Rundstedt and Blumentritt, elaborated their difficulties in conversation with Liddell Hart.*

The next question I explored was how the plan went wrong. Kleist's answer was: "The main cause of our failure was that winter came early that year, coupled with the way the Russians repeatedly gave ground rather than let themselves be drawn into a decisive battle such as we were seeking."

Rundstedt agreed that this was "the most decisive" cause. "But long before winter came, the chances had been diminished owing to the repeated delays in the advance that were caused by bad roads and mud. The black earth of the Ukraine could be turned into mud by ten minutes' rain – stopping all movement until it dried. That was a heavy handicap in a race with time. It was increased by the lack of railways in Russia – for bringing up supplies to our advancing troops. Another adverse factor was the way the Russians received continual reinforcements from their back areas, as they fell back. It seemed to us that as soon as one force was wiped out, the path was blocked by the arrival of a fresh force." . . .

General Blumentritt: "Although Field Marshal von Bock desired to continue the advance on Moscow, von Kluge did not share his view and was strongly in favour of the alternative plan of encircling the Russian forces around Kiev. It was his idea and desire that his own 4th Army should swing south to carry out this pincer movement along with Guderian's Panzer forces. When setting forth the arguments for this plan, he said to me with emphasis: 'It would also mean that *we* should be under Field Marshal von Rundstedt instead of Field Marshal von Bock'. Von Bock was a very difficult man to serve and von Kluge would have been glad to get out of his sphere. This was an interesting example of the influence of the personal factor in strategy."

Liddell Hart, B. H., *The Other Side of the Hill* (**54**), pp. 265, 275.

**document 6**
## The delay in the advance on Moscow

*By August 1941 Hitler was determined to switch his main thrust in Russia from Moscow to the Ukraine and the Crimea. This was regarded as a controversial decision by the generals, but such was his control that when General Guderian attended a conference at Army Group HQ on 23 August, he was ordered by Field Marshal von Brauchitsch not to mention Moscow to Hitler.*

On August 23 I was ordered to attend a conference at Army Group HQ, at which the chief of the Army General Staff was present. The latter informed us that Hitler had now decided that neither the Leningrad nor the Moscow operations would be carried out, but that the immediate objective should be the capture of the Ukraine and the Crimea. The Chief of the General Staff, Colonel-General Halder, seemed deeply upset at this shattering of his hopes, which were based on a resumption of the Moscow offensive. We discussed at length what could still be done to alter Hitler's 'unalterable resolve'. We were all agreed that this new plan to move on Kiev must result in a winter campaign; this in its turn would lead to all those difficulties which the OKH had very good reasons for wishing to avoid. I mentioned the road and supply problems which must arise if the tanks were to be sent south; I also expressed doubts as to the ability of our armoured equipment to perform these heavy new tasks as well as the subsequent winter advance on Moscow. I went on to draw attention to the condition of XXIV Panzer Corps, which had not had one single day for rest and maintenance since the opening of the Russian campaign . . .

I reported at once to the Commander-in-chief of the Army, Field Marshal von Brauchitsch, who greeted me with the following words: 'I forbid you to mention the question of Moscow to the Fuehrer. The operation to the south has been ordered. The problem now is simply how it is to be carried out. Discussion is pointless . . .'

I went in to see Hitler. There were a great many people present including Keitel, Jodl, Schmundt and others, but neither Brauchitsch nor Halder nor, indeed, any representative of the OKH. I described the state of my Panzer Group, its present condition and that of the terrain. When I had finished, Hitler asked: 'In view of their past performance, do you consider that your troops are capable of making another great effort?'

I replied: 'If the troops are given a major objective, the importance of which is apparent to every soldier, yes.'

Hitler then said: 'You mean, of course, Moscow.'

I answered: 'Yes. Since you have broached the subject, let me give you the reasons for my opinions.'

Hitler agreed and I therefore explained basically and in detail all the points that favoured a continuation of the advance on Moscow and that spoke against the Kiev operation . . .

Hitler let me speak to the end without once interrupting me. He then began to talk and described in detail the considerations which had led him to made a different decision. He said the raw materials and agriculture of the Ukraine were vitally necessary for the future prosecution of the war. He spoke once again of the need of neutralising the Crimea, 'that Soviet aircraft-carrier for attacking the Rumanian oilfields.' For the first time I heard him use the phrase: 'My generals know nothing about the economic aspects of war.'

Guderian, H., *Panzer Leader* (**48**) pp. 198, 199, 206.

## document 7
# Strategic considerations after the entry of the USA into the war

(**a**) *Immediately after the Japanese attack on Pearl Harbour in Hawaii in December 1941 had brought the United States into the war, Winston Churchill and a team of advisers crossed the Atlantic by sea in order to establish lasting arrangements with the American government which would ensure that the major effort was concentrated against Germany. During the course of the voyage Churchill composed three papers in which the proposal to make a landing in French North Africa in 1942 was put forward for the first time, and an Allied invasion of the Continent was suggested for 1943 (see p. 59).*

### The Atlantic front

4. We ought therefore to try hard to win over French North Africa, and now is the moment to use every inducement and form of pressure at our disposal upon the government of Vichy and French authorities in North Africa. The German setback in Russia, the British successes in Libya, the moral and military collapse of Italy, above all the declarations of war exchanged between Germany and the United States, must strongly affect the mind of France and the

French Empire. Now is the time to offer to Vichy and to French North Africa a blessing or a cursing. A blessing will consist in a promise by the United States and Great Britain to re-establish France as a great Power with her territories undiminished. It should carry with it an offer of active aid by British and United States expeditionary forces, both from the Atlantic seaboard of Morocco and at convenient landing-points in Algeria and Tunis, as well as from General Auchinleck's forces advancing from the east. Ample supplies for the French and the loyal Moors should be made available. Vichy should be asked to send their fleet from Toulon to Oran and Bizerta and to bring France into the war again as a principal . . .

### The campaign for 1943

5. We should therefore face now the problems not only of driving Japan back to her homelands and regaining undisputed mastery in the Pacific, but also of liberating conquered Europe by the landing during the summer of 1943 of United States and British armies on their shores. Plans should be prepared for the landing in all of the countries mentioned above. The actual choice of which three or four to pick should be deferred as long as possible, so as to profit by the turn of events and make sure of secrecy.

6. In principle, the landings should be made by armoured and mechanised forces capable of disembarking not at ports but on beaches, either by landing craft or from ocean-going ships specially adapted. The potential front of attack is thus made so wide that the German forces holding down these different countries cannot be strong enough at all points. An amphibious outfit must be prepared to enable these large scale embarkations to be made swiftly and surely.

Gwyer, J. M. A., *Grand Strategy* (**1b**), Vol 3, Part 1, pp. 326–7, 335.

(**b**) *After their meeting the British and American chiefs of staff eventually produced a combined statement largely in agreement with these proposals.*

*Memorandum by the United States and British Chiefs of Staff (WW1)*

### I. Grand Strategy

1. At the American-British conversations in February 1941 it was agreed that Germany was the predominant member of the Axis

Powers, and, consequently, the Atlantic and European area was considered to be the decisive theatre.

2. Much has happened since February last, but, notwithstanding the entry of Japan into the war, our view remains that Germany is still the prime enemy and her defeat is still the key to victory. Once Germany is defeated, the collapse of Italy and the defeat of Japan must follow.

3. In our considered opinion, therefore, it should be a cardinal principle of American-British strategy that only the minimum of force necessary for the safeguarding of vital interests in other theatres should be diverted from operations against Germany.

Closing and tightening the ring around Germany

13. This ring may be defined as a line running roughly as follows: Archangel – Black Sea – Anatolia – the northern seaboard of the Mediterranean – the western seaboard of Europe.

The main object will be to strengthen this ring, and close the gaps in it, by sustaining the Russian front, by arming and supporting Turkey, by increasing our strength in the Middle East, and by gaining possession of the whole North African coast.

14. If this ring can be closed, the blockade of Germany and Italy will be complete, and German eruptions, e.g. towards the Persian Gulf, or the Atlantic seaboard of Africa, will be prevented. Furthermore, the seizing of the North African coast may open the Mediterranean to convoys, thus enormously shortening the route to the Middle East and saving considerable tonnage now employed in the long haul round the Cape.

17. In 1943 the way may be clear for a return to the Continent, across the Mediterranean, from Turkey into the Balkans, or by landings in Western Europe. Such operations must be the prelude to the final assault on Germany itself, and the scope of the victory programme should be such as to provide means by which they can be carried out.

Howard, Michael, *Grand Strategy* (**1b**) Vol 4, pp. 597, 599.

(c) *To General Marshall, the American Army Chief of Staff, however, these plans were too diverse to allow the necessary concentration of forces and ignored the potential of Great Britain as a jumping-off ground for an immediate invasion of the Continent. Accordingly, in March 1942 he submitted the following memorandum to the American President (see p. 60).*

Western Europe has been selected as the theatre in which to stage the first great offensive of the United Powers because:

It is the only place in which a powerful offensive can be prepared and executed by the United Powers in the near future. In any other locality the building up of the required forces would be much more slowly accomplished due to sea distances. Moreover, in other localities the enemy is protected against invasion by natural obstacles and poor communications leading to the seat of the hostile Power, or by elaborately organized and distant outposts. Time would be required to reduce these and to make the attack effective.

It is the only place where the vital air superiority over the hostile land areas preliminary to a major attack can be staged by the United Powers. This is due to the existence of a network of landing fields in England and to the fact that at no other place could massed British air power be employed for such an operation.

It is the only place in which the bulk of the British ground forces can be committed to a general offensive in cooperation with United States forces. It is impossible, in view of the shipping situation, to transfer the bulk of the British forces to any distant region, and the protection of the British islands would hold the bulk of the divisions in England.

The United States can concentrate and use larger forces in Western Europe than in any other place, due to sea distances and the existence in England of base facilities.

The bulk of the combat forces of the United States, United Kingdom and Russia can be applied simultaneously only against Germany, and then only if we attack in time. We cannot concentrate against Japan.

Successful attack in this area will afford the maximum of support to the Russian front.

Sherwood, Robert E., *Roosevelt and Hopkins, an intimate history* (**63**), pp. 519–20

## The survival of Malta

document 8

*One of the most remarkable circumstances during the war in the Mediterranean was that Malta never fell to the Axis Powers and remained an active base from which the Allies could constantly attack the supply convoys for the Afrika Korps in North Africa. The effectiveness of these attacks was greatly increased through information on the composition of the convoys supplied by the Intelligence unit at Bletchley (see p. 50). Malta was heavily bombed and endured many months of siege, but Hitler never attempted a landing, and after the war Liddell Hart discussed the reasons for this with General Student.*

General Student: A year later, however, he [Hitler] was persuaded to adopt a plan for capturing Malta. This was in April 1942. The attack was to be carried out in conjunction with the Italians. My airborne forces, together with the Italian ones, were to be dropped on the island and capture a bridgehead which would then be re-inforced by a large Italian sea-borne force – of six to eight divisions. My force comprised our one existing parachute division, three additional regiments that had not yet been organized as a division, and an Italian parachute division.

I had hoped to carry out the plan not later than August – it depended on suitable weather – and spent some months in Rome preparing it. In June I was summoned to Hitler's headquarters for the final conference on the operation. Unfortunately, the day before I got there, Hitler had seen General Crüwell, who was just back from North Africa, and had been given a very unfavourable account of the state of the Italian forces and their morale.

Hitler at once took alarm. He felt that if the British fleet appeared on the scene, all the Italian ships would bolt for their home ports – and leave the German airborne forces stranded. He decided to abandon the plan of attacking Malta.

Liddell Hart, B. H., *The Other Side of the Hill* (**54**), p. 243.

**document 9**
# Churchill and Stalin in Moscow: August 1942

*After the German attack in June 1941 the Russians demanded a cross-Channel invasion to establish a second front which would relieve the pressure on their own forces. It has been seen (p. 60) that after their entry into the war the Americans, too, believed that an invasion might be possible in 1942, but the British chiefs of staff were adamant that this would be premature. It was vital, however, that the Russians should not be discouraged. Thus the landings in North-West Africa were set in motion as a substitute for invasion, and Churchill flew to Moscow to explain this personally to Stalin, who eventually warmed to the scheme. Sir Alan Brooke, chief of the imperial general staff and chairman of the Combined Chiefs of Staff committee, wrote this account of the meeting afterwards.*

It had been a long and tiring flight lasting some fifteen hours. I was longing for a bath, light dinner and bed. It was not to be – as I stepped out of the plane, I was handed a message from Winston to come at once to dine with him, to go on to the Kremlin at 11 p.m.

Tired as I was, I would not have missed that meeting between Stalin and Winston for anything in the world. Everything of that meeting is still vivid in my memory. We were shown into a sparsely furnished room of the Kremlin, which reminded me of a station waiting-room. I think the only picture on the wall was that of Lenin. Stalin, Molotov, and the interpreter entered and we sat at a long table.

We were soon involved in heated discussions concerning the Western Second Front, and Winston had made it clear that such an offensive was not possible for the present, but would be replaced by operations in North Africa. Stalin then began to turn on the heat, and through the interpreter he passed a lot of abusive questions such as: "When are you going to start fighting? Are you going to let us do all the work whilst you look on? Are you never going to start fighting? You will find that it is not too bad, if you once start" etc., etc.

The effect on Winston was magnetic. He crashed his fist down on the table and poured forth one of his wonderful spontaneous orations. It began with: "If it was not for the fighting qualities of the Red Army . . ." And then went on to tell Stalin exactly what his feelings were about fighting and a lot more.

Stalin stood up sucking at his large bent pipe and with a broad grin on his face stopped Winston's interpreter and sent back through his own: "I do not understand what you are saying, but by God I like your sentiment."

Looking back on that episode, I am convinced that Stalin insulted Winston with the purpose of finding out what his reactions would be, of sizing up what kind of a man he was. He very soon discovered what Winston was made of, and I am certain that this outburst of Winston's had impressed Stalin and started feelings of admiration for what he discovered was a true fighting man. At any rate, from that moment onwards the relations between the two improved and there grew up between them certain bonds of mutual admiration and appreciation based on the highly developed fighting qualities which both of them possessed.

Bryant, A., *The Turn of the Tide 1939–1943* (**35**), pp. 380–1.

## document 10
# Stalingrad: November 1942

*In conversation with Liddell Hart, the German general Warlimont comments here on the fatal decision to concentrate on the taking of Stalingrad (see p. 25).*

I am convinced that Hitler, when confronted with the actual situation at the end of the second offensive against Russia, suddenly grasped that he would never reach his goal in the East and that the war would eventually be lost.

The danger arising from the long-stretched flank west of Stalingrad was evident also to Hitler, particularly because he came to know somehow that it was Stalin himself who had been behind the decisive blow which the Reds administered to the 'White Guards' in that region in a rather similar situation of 1919.

In addition, it became known that the Rumanian divisions, then gradually filling up the defensive front west of Stalingrad, were most inadequately equipped – marching up there from the far-distant railheads, partly without even shoes on their bare feet. Hitler, however, consciously faced the growing danger, trusting that a quick capture of Stalingrad would set free sufficient German forces to relieve the tense situation. But, instead, more and more German troops, finally even single battalions, were drawn away from the defensive wing in order to strengthen the desperate efforts at Stalingrad. At the same time the Russian counter-offensive against Army Group Centre, particularly in the Rzhev area, became a serious threat and caused increasing casualties. It was on this issue that the final clash between Hitler and Halder originated, which led to the latter's dismissal.

Liddell Hart, B. H., *The Other Side of the Hill* (**54**), p. 315.

## document 11
# Decision at Casablanca: January 1943

*After the victory at El Alamein and the successful landings in Morocco and Algeria, the western Allies met at Casablanca in January 1943. Here Brooke was determined to continue with a Mediterranean strategy that might eventually knock Italy out of the war (see p. 62), and this extract from his diary recounts the occasion when agreement was finally reached on this. The references are to Admiral King, commander-in-chief of the American navy; to Sir*

*John Dill, head of the British military delegation at Washington; and to Sir Charles Portal, chief of the British air staff.*

*January 18* . . . From 10.30 to 1 p.m. a very heated Combined Chiefs of Staff meeting at which we seemed to be making no progress. King still evidently wrapped up in the war of the Pacific at the expense of everything else. However, immediately after lunch I sat down with Dill, I must confess without much hope, trying to define the line of our general agreement. In the middle Portal came in with a better paper. I therefore decided on the spur of the moment, and without a chance of seeing the First Sea Lord, to try and use this proposed policy as a bridge over our difficulties.

We met again at 3 p.m. and I produced our paper which was accepted with few alterations. I could hardly believe our luck.

Shortly afterwards we were informed that the President would hold a full meeting with the P.M. and all Combined Chiefs of Staff to hear results we had reached. We met at his villa at 5.30 p.m. I was asked to sit next to him, and he asked me who had been acting as our Chairman and I informed him that Marshall had been invited by us to perform that function. He then called on Marshall who at once asked me to expound the results of our meetings. It was a difficult moment. We had only just succeeded in getting the American Chiefs of Staff to agree with us. However, the statement went all right, was approved by the Americans and the President and P.M. and received a full blessing. So we have reached some results after all.

Bryant, A., *The Turn of the Tide 1939–1943* (**35**), p. 453

**document 12**

# Unconditional surrender

*A further decision taken at Casablanca and issued to the press immediately was that the Allies would only accept unconditional surrender from their enemies, and there has been considerable controversy over whether this demand unnecessarily prolonged the war (see p. 65).*

*President Roosevelt*: Another point, I think we had all had it in our hearts and heads before, but I don't think that it has ever been put down on paper by the Prime Minister and myself, and that is the determination that peace can come to the world only by the total elimination of German and Japanese war power.

Some of you Britishers know the old story – we had a General U.S. Grant. His name was Ulysses Simpson Grant, but in my, and the Prime Minister's early days, he was called 'Unconditional Surrender' Grant. The elimination of German, Japanese and Italian war power means the unconditional surrender by Germany, Japan and Italy. This means a reasonable assurance of future world peace. It does not mean the destruction of the population of Germany, Italy or Japan, but it does mean the destruction of the philosophies in those countries which are based on conquest and the subjugation of other peoples.

Howard, Michael, *Grand Strategy* (**1b**), vol 4, pp. 281–2.

**document 13**

# The fall of Mussolini: July 1943

*On 25 July 1943, a fortnight after the Allied landing in Sicily, Mussolini was removed from power by the Italian Grand Council and placed under arrest. Marshal Badoglio was appointed head of a new government. The problem for the Italians was that if they were now to change sides, they must be able to reach agreement secretly with the Allies, before the Germans carried out an occupation. In fact, no agreement was reached until September, by which time Field Marshal Kesselring had disbanded the Italian army and was ready to form a front against the Allied invasion of south Italy. The demand for unconditional surrender has sometimes been blamed for this delay, but this was by no means the only problem (see p. 65). Indeed, from this record of Hitler's conference on the day of Mussolini's fall, it is clear that Hitler had grasped the danger at once and was determined to take action.*

*General Jodl*: The decisive thing is: are the Italians going to continue fighting or not?
*Hitler*: They say they will fight, but it is certainly treachery. We must realise that this is open treachery . . .
. . . Although that so-and-so [Badoglio] declared immediately that the war would be continued, that won't make any difference. They have to say that, but it remains treason. But we'll play the same game while preparing everything to take over the whole crew with one stroke, to capture all of that riffraff. Tomorrow I'll send a man down there with orders for the commander of the Third Panzergrenadier Division to the effect that he must drive into Rome with a special detail and arrest the whole government, the

King and the whole bunch right away. First of all, to arrest the
Crown Prince and to take over the whole gang, especially Badoglio
and that entire crew. Then watch them cave in, and in two or three
days there'll be another coup . . .

Gilbert, F. (ed.), *Hitler Directs His War* (**27**), pp. 48, 50–1.

# document 14
# The possibility of an Allied victory in autumn 1944

*The following comment was made to Liddell Hart by General Blumentritt
after the war. It echoes the statement often made by German generals that
the Allies could have broken into Germany from the west in the autumn of
1944. It was only natural for them to claim this, since if the Allies had
succeeded in doing so, there would probably, although not certainly, have been
no partition of Germany. Their argument, however, does ignore the logistical
problem, which normally dictates a lull after a major offensive has run its
course – as it often did on the Russian front; it also ignores the remarkable
power of recovery demonstrated by the German themselves, supremely illus-
trated by the Ardennes counter-attack in December 1944.*

*Blumentritt*: The best course of the Allies would have been to
concentrate a really strong striking force with which to break
through past Aachen to the Ruhr area. Strategically and politically, Berlin was the target. Germany's strength is in the north.
South Germany was a side issue. He who holds northern Germany
holds Germany. Such a break-through, coupled with air domination, would have torn in pieces the weak German front and ended
the war. Berlin and Prague would have been occupied ahead of the
Russians. There were no German forces behind the Rhine, and at
the end of August our front was wide open.

There was an operational break-through in the Aachen area in
September. This facilitated a rapid conquest of the Ruhr and a
quicker advance on Berlin. By turning the forces from the Aachen
area sharply northward, the German 15th and 1st Parachute
Armies could have been pinned against the estuaries of the Maas
and the Rhine. They could not have escaped eastwards into
Germany.

Liddell Hart, B. H., *The Other Side of the Hill* (**54**), p. 428.

# The final surrenders

*This is a transcript of a telephone conversation across the Atlantic between Churchill and Truman, President of the United States since Roosevelt's death in April 1945. It took place at the very end of the war, and its untidiness conveys very well the sense of excitement at the imminent collapse, the speed at which things were happening, and the need to find some way of coping with the massive surrenders, as the Allied armies closed in. It also shows how to the end the western Allies were determined to preserve their agreements with Russia in defiance of Hitler's last remaining hope that these would break down.*

*Churchill* (reading out a report from the British ambassador at Stockholm that the Swedes had been approached by Himmler about a German surrender in the west.) 'I wrote that my United States colleague and I remarked that in reference to the Axis' unwillingness to surrender on the eastern front looks like a last attempt to sow discord between the western Allies and Russia. Obviously the Nazis would have to surrender to all the Allies simultaneously'.

*Truman*: That is right. That is exactly the way I feel. He ought to surrender to all the Allies at once.

*Churchill*: 'The Minister for Foreign Affairs and Government, while admitting that this motive could not be excluded, pointed out that the fact that the Nazi chiefs would order capitulation of all troops on the whole of the western front and in Norway and Denmark, might be of great advantage for all the Allies, including Russia, and would in fact lead to early total capitulation.'(These are all the Swedes talking.) 'And they say in any case, the Minister for Foreign Affairs hoped to clear this up, this provision. He said, pass it on to the British and United States governments who were, as far as the Swedish government were concerned, at complete liberty to transmit it to the Soviet government. That the Swedish government would in no way be, or propose to be, an instrument in promoting any attempt to sow discord between the Allies. The only reason for not informing the Soviet government directly was because Himmler had stipulated that this information was exclusively for the western Allies.' (He said that if the United States colleague is sending a telegram to say so.) Of course we are not bound by that, and it's our duty to tell Stalin, in my opinion.

*Truman*: I think so too. Have you notified Stalin?

*Churchill*: I held it up for about two hours, hoping to get an answer to the telegram I sent you, but I have now released the telegram. This is the telegram I have sent.

*Truman*: All right, then you notify Stalin and I shall do the same immediately of this conversation between us.

*Churchill*: Exactly. Here is what I have said to Stalin and I have telegraphed it over to you. The telegram immediately following is one I have just received exactly from the British ambassador in Sweden. 'The President of the United States has the news also.' I thought you had gotten it. Your telegram has not gotten through.

*Truman*: No, I haven't received my telegram as yet.

*Churchill*: 'There can be no question as far as His Majesty's government is concerned, arranging thus an unconditional surrender simultaneously to the three major Powers'.

*Truman*: I agree to that fully.

*Churchill*: 'We consider Himmler should be told that German folk either as individuals or in units should everywhere surrender themselves to the Allied troops or representatives on the spot. Until this happens, the attack of the Allies upon them on all sides and in all theatres where resistance continues will be prosecuted with the utmost vigour.'

Truman, H. S., *Year of Decisions 1945* (**43**), pp. 94–6.

# Bibliography

OFFICIAL HISTORIES
**1a** Butler, Sir James (ed.), *History of the Second World War*, United Kingdom, Military series, HMSO.
**1b** *Grand Strategy*, 6 vols. 1956–76.
**2** Ellis, L. F., *France and Flanders 1939–40*, 1954.
**3** Ellis, L. F., *Victory in the West*, 2 vols. 1962, 1968.
**4** Playfair, I. S. O., *The Mediterranean and the Middle East*, 6 vols. 1954–73.
**5** Roskill, S. W., *The War at Sea*, 3 vols. 1954–60.
**6** Webster, C. and Frankland, A. N., *The Strategic Air Offensive*, 4 vols. 1961.
**7** Foot, M. R. D., *S. O. E. in France*, HMSO, 1966.
**8** Richards, D., *Royal Air Force 1939–1945*, 3 vols. HMSO, 1953–54.
**9** Woodward, L., *British Foreign Policy in the Second World War*, 5 vols. HMSO, 1961.


OTHER HISTORIES
**10** Fuller, J. F. C., *The Second World War. 1939–1945*, Eyre & Spottiswood, 1954.
**11** Liddell Hart, B. H., *History of the Second World War*, Cassell, 1970.
**12** Parkinson, R., *Peace in our Time*, Hart Davis, MacGibbon, 1971.
**13** Parkinson, R., *Blood, Tears, Toil and Sweat*, Hart Davis, MacGibbon, 1973.
**14** Parkinson, R., *A Day's March Nearer Home*, Hart Davis, MacGibbon, 1974.
**15** Wilmot, C., *The Struggle for Europe*, Collins, 1952.
**16** Lewin, R., *Ultra Goes To War*, Hutchinson, 1978.
**17** Winterbotham, F. W., *The Ultra Secret*, Weidenfeld & Nicolson, 1974.
**18** Jones, R. V., *Most Secret War*, Hamish Hamilton, 1978.

**19**  Grigg, J., *1943: The Victory That Never Was*, Eyre Methuen, 1980.

**20**  Douglas, R., *From War to Cold War 1942–1948*, Macmillan, 1981.

**21**  Reynolds, D., *The Creation of the Anglo-American Alliance 1937–41*, Europa, 1981.

GERMANY

**22**  Cooper, M., *The German Army 1933–1945*, Macdonald & Jane's, 1978.

**23**  Cooper, M., *The German Air Force 1933–1945*, Jane's, 1981.

**24**  Craig, G., *Germany 1866–1945*, Oxford University Press, 1978.

**25**  Craig, G., *The Politics of the Prussian Army 1640–1945*, Oxford University Press, 1955.

**26**  van Crefeld, Martin, *Hitler's Strategy 1940–1941, the Balkan Clue*, Cambridge University Press, 1973.

**27**  Gilbert, F. (ed.), *Hitler Directs His War: Records of his Daily Conferences*, Oxford University Press, 1950.

**28**  Hinsley, F. H., *Hitler's Strategy*, Cambridge University Press, 1951.

**29**  Hitler, A., *Hitler's Table Talk 1941–44*, ed. H. R. Trevor-Roper, Weidenfeld & Nicolson, 1953.

**30**  Hitler, A., *Hitler's War Directives 1939–1945*, ed. H. R. Trevor-Roper, Sidgwick & Jackson, 1964.

**31**  Milward, A. S., *The German Economy at War*, Athlone Press, 1965.

**32**  Shirer, W. L., *The Rise and Fall of the Third Reich*, Secker & Warburg, 1960.

**33**  Westphal, S. (ed.), *The Fatal Decisions*, Michael Joseph, 1956.

**34**  Wheeler-Bennett, J., *The Nemesis of Power*, Macmillan, 1953.

MEMOIRS

*British*

**35**  Bryant, A., *The Turn of the Tide 1939–1943*, (1957); *Triumph in the West* (1959), Collins, (the diaries of Field Marshal Viscount Alanbrooke).

**36**  Churchill, W. S., *History of the Second World War*, 6 vols, Cassell, 1948–54.

**37**  Guingand, Sir Francis de, *Operation Victory*, Hodder & Stoughton, 1947.

**38**  Maclean, F., *Eastern Approaches*, Cape, 1949.

**39** Montgomery, B. L., *The Memoirs of Field Marshal Montgomery*, Collins, 1958.

**40** Spears, L., *Assignment to Catastrophe*, 2 vols., Heinemann, 1954.

*American*

**41** Butcher, H. C., *My Three Years With Eisenhower*, Heinemann, 1946.

**42** Eisenhower, D. D., *Crusade in Europe*, Heinemann, 1949.

**43** Truman, H. S., *Year of Decisions 1945*, Hodder & Stoughton, 1955.

*French*

**44** de Gaulle, C., *The Call to Honour 1940–42*, Collins, 1955.

**45** de Gaulle, C., *Unity 1942–44*, Collins 1956.

**46** Weygand, M., *Recalled to Service*, Heinemann, 1952.

*Italian*

**47** Ciano, Count Galeazzo, *Diaries 1939–43*, ed. M. Muggeridge, Heinemann, 1957.

*German*

**48** Guderian, H., *Panzer Leader*, Michael Joseph, 1952.

**49** Halder, F., *Hitler as War Lord*, Putnam, 1950.

**50** Rommel, E., *The Rommel Papers*, ed. B. H. Liddell Hart, Collins, 1953.

**51** Speer, A., *Inside the Third Reich*, Weidenfeld & Nicolson, 1970.

**52** Speidel, H., *We Defended Normandy*, Jenkins, 1951.

**53** Warlimont, W., *Inside Hitler's Headquarters 1939–1945*, New York, 1964.

**54** Liddell Hart, B. H., *The Other Side of the Hill*, Cassell, 1951.

BIOGRAPHIES (Alphabetical by subject)

**55** Fraser, D., *Alanbrooke*, Collins, 1982.

**56** Bullock, A., *Hitler: a study in tyranny*, Odhams 1952.

**57** Fest, J. C., *Hitler*, Pelican, 1977.

**58** Strawson, J., *Hitler as Military Commander*, Batsford, 1971.

**59** Deakin, F. W., *The Brutal Friendship*, Penguin, 1966.

**60** Deakin, F. W., *The Last Days of Mussolini*, Penguin, 1966.

**61** Richards, D., *Portal of Hungerford*, Heinemann, 1977.

**62** Young, D., *Rommel*, Collins, 1950.

**63** Sherwood, R. E., *Roosevelt and Hopkins: an intimate history*, Harper & Row, 1950.

*Bibliography*

**64**   Deutscher I., *Stalin*, Oxford University Press, 1949.
**65**   Connell, J., *Wavell, Scholar and Soldier*, Collins, 1964.
**66**   Connell, J., *Wavell, Supreme Commander 1941–43*, Collins, 1969.
**67**   Barnett, C., *The Desert Generals*, Allen & Unwin, 1983.

CAMPAIGNS

*France 1940*
**68**   Benoist-Méchlin, J., *Sixty Days That Shook The World*, Cape, 1963.
**69**   Fleming, P., *Invasion 1940*, Pan, 1975.
**70**   Horne, A., *To Lose A Battle*, Macmillan, 1969.

*The Mediterranean Theatre*
**71**   Jackson, W. G. F., *The North African Campaign 1940–43*, Batsford, 1975.
**72**   Lewin, R., *The Life and Death of the Afrika Korps*, Batsford, 1977.
**73**   Pitt, B., *The Crucible of War: Western Desert 1941*, Cape, 1980.

*Russia*
**74**   Clark, A., *Barbarossa*, Penguin, 1966.
**75**   Dunnigan, J. F. (ed.), *The Russian Front*, Arms and Armour Press, 1978.
**76**   Erickson, J., *The Road to Stalingrad*, Weidenfeld & Nicolson, 1975.
**77**   Erickson, J., *The Road to Berlin*, Weidenfeld & Nicolson, 1983.
**78**   Seaton, A., *The Russo-German War 1941–1945*, Barker, 1971.
**79**   Werth, A., *Russia at War 1941–1945*, Barrie & Rockliff, 1964.

*Normandy*
**80**   Belfield, E. and Essame, H., *The Battle for Normandy*, Batsford, 1965.
**81**   d'Este, C., *Decision in Normandy*, Collins, 1983.
**82**   Hastings, Max, *Overlord. D. Day and the battle for Normandy 1944*, Michael Joseph, 1984.
**83**   Keegan, J., *Six Armies in Normandy*, Penguin, 1983.
(See also a detailed account in Wilmot, C., *The Struggle for Europe* (**15**).

*The last stages*
**84**   Essame, H., *The Battle for Germany*, Batsford, 1969.

110

**85** Ryan, C., *A Bridge Too Far*, Hamilton, 1974 (about Arnhem).
**86** Ryan, C., *The Last Battle*, Collins 1966 (about Berlin, 1945).

ARTICLES IN PERIODICALS
**87** Hillgrüber, A., 'England's Place in Hitler's Plan for World Domination', *Journal of Contemporary History*, January 1974.
**88** Stolfi, R. H. S., 'Equipment for Victory in France in 1940', *History*, lv (1970).
**89** Stolfi, R. H. S., 'Chance in History: The Russian Winter of 1941–42', *History*, lxv (1980).

# Index

# Index

Rhine river, 36, 38, 82
Ribbentrop, J von, 64, 91
Rokossovski, Marshal C., 27, 80
Rome, 29, 65
Rommel, General E., 17, 23–4, 25, 28, 29, 32, 78, 84
Roosevelt, President Franklin D., 17, 22, 29, 56, 59–61, 65, 69, 70, 75, 76, 83, 102, 103, 105
Rotterdam, 9, 44
Ruhr, The, 38, 43, 77
Rundstedt, Field Marshal C. R. G. von, 7, 9, 13, 20, 32, 33, 35, 69, 89, 93
Russia, 20–2, 25–6, 27–8, 35–6, 38, 57–8, 90, 91, 92, 93, 94
Russian army, 5–6, 20–2

Salerno, 29
Scheldt, The, 9, 36, 37, 81, 82
Sebastopol, 25–8
Sedan, 11
Sicily, 29, 62
Sidi Barrani, 17
Singapore, 22, 77
Smolensk, 20, 21, 28, 59
Spain, 72
Speer, Albert, 44, 53, 54, 55
Stalin, 64, 83, 99–100, 101
Stalingrad, 25, 26, 64, 78, 101
Student, General K., 19, 81, 82, 99
Suez canal, 23
Sweden 8, 9, 105

Taranto, 17
Thomas, General Georg, 53
Tobruk, 23, 24
Todt, Fritz, 54
Torch, Operation, 24–5, 60, 61
Toulon, 25
Truman, President Harry S., 105–6
Tunis, 28, 29

Ukraine, The, 20, 21, 94
Ultra, 3, 15, 19, 23, 28, 35, 50
United States of America, 22, 47–8, 56–7, 59–61, 95–8

V1, V2, 31, 49, 52
Vichy, 17, 24, 96
Vistula river, 8, 36, 38, 59, 67, 79
Voronezh, 25

Warsaw, 8, 38, 44, 80
Wavell, General Sir Archibald, 17, 23, 72
Weizsaecker, E. von, 91
Wesel, 40
West Indies, 47, 70
Weygand, General M., 11
Wilmot, Chester, 63, 66, 80

Yalta, 40, 80
Yugoslavia, 19, 73, 74

114